MW00344720

Start, Stop, or Grow?

ROBERT GRAY ATKINS

Start, Stop, or Grow?

**A DATA-INFORMED APPROACH TO
ACADEMIC PROGRAM EVALUATION AND MANAGEMENT**

Advantage

Published by Advantage, Charleston, South Carolina.
Member of Advantage Media Group.

ADVANTAGE is a registered trademark, and the Advantage colophon is a trademark of Advantage Media Group, Inc.

Printed in the United States of America.

10 9 8 7 6 5 4 3 2 1

ISBN: 978-1-64225-270-5
LCCN: 2022905015

Cover design by Megan Elger.
Layout design by Wesley Strickland.

This publication is designed to provide accurate and authoritative information in regard to the subject matter covered. It is sold with the understanding that the publisher is not engaged in rendering legal, accounting, or other professional services. If legal advice or other expert assistance is required, the services of a competent professional person should be sought.

Advantage Media Group is proud to be a part of the Tree Neutral® program. Tree Neutral offsets the number of trees consumed in the production and printing of this book by taking proactive steps such as planting trees in direct proportion to the number of trees used to print books. To learn more about Tree Neutral, please visit **www.treeneutral.com**.

Advantage Media Group is a publisher of business, self-improvement, and professional development books and online learning. We help entrepreneurs, business leaders, and professionals share their Stories, Passion, and Knowledge to help others Learn & Grow. Do you have a manuscript or book idea that you would like us to consider for publishing? Please visit **advantagefamily.com**.

To my wife, with all my love.

Thank you to my partners, Mary Upchurch, Steve Probst, Pete Starrett, and Zach Paz, whose friendship, professionalism, and leadership have made Gray the greatest adventure and creation of my life.

Thank you to all the members of the Gray team, past and present, who have helped develop the facts, methods, and insights that are the foundation of this book—with special thanks to Elaine for countless hours of researching, writing, and editing client reports, proposals, and this book.

And finally, to the hundreds of career and technical colleges, liberal arts colleges, and universities, clients who have placed their trust in Gray and made our journey possible. I hope this book helps you thrive and lead the world in educational excellence and equity.

Contents

Foreword

Start, Stop, or Grow? presents an exciting new approach to academic program evaluation and management. It systematically brings markets and money into the decision-making equation, alongside consideration of institutional mission, academic standards, and student success. What Bob Atkins describes is both conceptually innovative and eminently practical. Readers will expand their thinking about how to approach the perennial problems of academic planning and budget-making. They will learn about a new class of tools that can provide the needed information, quickly and accessibly, at a surprisingly modest cost. This short book promises to be a game changer for academic resourcing.

What information is needed when deciding whether to start, stop, or grow a particular degree program? Traditionally, decision makers focus on factors such as the qualifications of students and faculty and the availability of appropriate facilities and infrastructure (e.g., library resources, IT, and laboratories). Fit with the institution's mission is important as well, as is the ability to fund the necessary staffing and operating costs. But these factors present only part of the story. Missing are data on the fine structure of student demand, competition, and what is coming to be called "program economics." The latter should not be confused with financial measures as compiled by the business office (e.g., what's captured in the general ledger). It centers on *structural representations* of academic activities, student revenues and discounts, average and incremental instructional costs, and margins—all captured at the level of individual programs, courses, sections, and academic departments. Getting these measures requires detailed data collection and modeling, and the book provides many "how-to" examples for both.

Suppose your institution is considering whether to grow its psychology program, for example, perhaps to help erase a looming budget deficit. Whether the school will be able to attract the additional qualified students is a threshold question, which in turn depends on the demand for psychology graduates and the market potential and competition in your relevant market geography. (There is a wealth of available data, but it's not easy to acquire and process without a model. For example, most psych majors go into fields other than psychology.) Let's assume the expansion fits well with mission and that the requisite facilities and infrastructure can be made available. The question, then, is whether the expansion will pay for itself or, if not, whether the degree of subsidy required will be affordable and consistent with other priorities.

Simple calculations based on business office data might show that the cost per credit hour taught in the Psychology Department (i.e., the total departmental cost divided by total credit hours) is high, but that doesn't mean the cost of a psychology degree will be high. An economic model might reveal that many of the extra psychology credits would be earned in existing courses without proportional additions to section counts. Such synergies produce significant cost savings, which might well be amplified because a substantial number of psychology student credits are earned in departments that are inherently less costly. This simple but realistic example shows that good economic analyses are not a "nice things to have" when making program growth decisions but rather not doing them risks making poor choices.

The prior example is instructive, but it does not directly address the critical concept of "academic tradeoffs." This reflects the universal truth that, in an environment with resource constraints, one cannot always get everything one wants. It's necessary to "trade off" one good against another, so as not to fail financially or incur some other serious penalty. Tradeoffs require that the range of alternatives be considered holistically—in this case as a "portfolio" of programs instead of as individual programs in isolation. Suppose, in the example, that there is an overall limit on the college's total student population—as might be caused, say, by constraints on dormitory spaces or some other element of institutional capacity. This limitation means that growing some programs will require shrinking or stopping others. Now, the decision is more complicated and has higher stakes, which makes the market and economic factors even more important

Start, Stop, or Grow? presumes that provosts, deans, program heads, department chairs, and faculty will internalize the elements of market and program economics that impact decisions in their areas. This is a change from traditional practice. Traditionally, academic leaders view their responsibilities through the lens of institutional mission, academic standards, and student success. Market and economic factors are considered less deeply and delegated to enrollment management and financial professionals whenever possible.

Such delegation is dangerous in a fast-changing and resource-constrained environment. The danger stems from the intrinsic nature of academic tradeoff decisions, i.e., that mission, standard-keeping, and student success cannot be separated cleanly from markets and economics. The decision maker must weigh all the factors together—even though, as one might say, they include apples, oranges, and cumquats.

Academic decision makers whose judgments do not deeply consider the market and economic factors put their institutions at significant risk, both financially and for lost educational and research opportunities. They also create a vacuum in which nonacademic professionals, especially financial officers, may play an outsized role in academic decision-making—if for no other reason than to forfend financial ruin. These risks have always been present, but they are more urgent in today's environment.

Bob Atkins offers solutions to this problem. The data systems and models he describes are based on extensive work that he and his colleagues have done at a wide variety of colleges and universities. They are state of the art and, just as importantly, are accessible and actionable for provosts, deans, and other academic leaders who are willing to engage with them. It turns out that, as academic officers and faculty dig more deeply into the models, their confidence in them tends to increase. Purely financial models and data can't pass this test, but I have observed the phenomenon in my own work that faculty are likely to trust systems that model the *activities* associated with programs, courses, and departments rather than financial quantities only.

There are, of course, barriers to adopting such academic decision support models. The main problem does not stem from a lack of intention. Universities want to do better, but too often their efforts are overwhelmed by other priorities. Complacency and resistance to change also play a role. However, the root causes stem from a deeply held commitment to traditional concepts and values and a worry that, eventually, using the models to evaluate instructional costs and margins will drive out considerations of quality.

Bob addresses these barriers directly. The approaches he describes consider the nature and purposes of an institution's academic activity in a balanced way—with special emphasis on the area of instruction. The models have the transparency and understandability needed for acceptance. The sufficient condition is that they actually help users make better decisions. The improvements are apparent to anyone who looks at them with an open mind.

Start, Stop, or Grow? furthers the vision I laid out in *Reengineering the University* and *Resource Management for Colleges and Universities* (Johns Hopkins University Press, 2016 and 2020). I've worked with Gray Associates as they developed software and expertise in the areas I wrote about, along with many others of their own creation. The book reduces the key ideas to practice, reports on successful applications, and previews some of the innovations that are likely to emerge in the near future.

Change is never easy in academe, and the improvement of academic program evaluation and management is no exception. The pages you are about to read will point the way forward, both conceptually and in terms that are imminently practical.

William F. Massy
Professor Emeritus and former Vice Provost for Research and Vice President for Business and Finance, Stanford University; Senior Consultant with Gray Associates

Introduction

This is a short book by a small team in a small company. Its topic is limited to academic program evaluation and management in higher education. While narrow, this topic has an enormous impact. Program evaluations affect what generations of students will learn, what skills they will develop, the success they will have at work, and how they will contribute to society. Evaluations change the institutions themselves, driving academic costs—who will be hired and let go, what research will be done, and who will be included in our campus communities—and guiding how our science, culture, and ethics will be handed down from one generation to the next.

The foundations of program evaluation and management are under severe stress. Human knowledge is increasing, university budgets are falling, critics are ever more passionate, students and their preferences are more diverse, and common approaches to evaluation are rusty and divisive.

The body of human knowledge—what may need to be taught—is greater than ever before. By some accounts, it is doubling every thirteen months; a more conservative view is that knowledge is growing about 4 percent per year,[1] the approximate growth rate for patents issued in the US and for worldwide scholarly articles.

In the face of this rising tide, the resources available to teach are growing more slowly (3 percent annually)[2] or being cut by state governments, enrollment declines, and a recent pandemic. The gap between the growth in knowledge and budgets poses a fundamental challenge: What should we teach?

There are passionate advocates for and against many programs. One central issue is the balance between career-focused training and more traditional liberal arts and sciences. Many people and politicians have strong opinions, often with no knowledge of the content of programs or their career outcomes. My favorite example is the ridicule of philosophy programs as a waste of time and money that produce unemployable graduates: "Welders make more money than philosophers. We need more welders and less philosophers."[3] According to this logic, colleges should do more training and less educating.

The statement and the underlying reasoning are incorrect. The average welder makes about $44,190.[4] Before age thirty, philosophy majors' income is about the same as welders. By midcareer, philosophy majors average $96,000 per year in income—more than double the wages for welders. However, philosophy majors usually do not go

1   David Russell Schilling, "Knowledge Doubling Every 12 Months, Soon to Be Every 12 Hours," Industry Tap, April 19, 2013, https://www.industrytap.com/knowledge-doubling-every-12-months-soon-to-be-every-12-hours/3950.

2   Gray analysis of the Integrated Postsecondary Education Data System (IPEDS) total instructional cost, 2009–2019.

3   Gregory Krieg, "Marco Rubio's Quip about Welders Gets Torched," CNN, November 11, 2015, https://www.cnn.com/2015/11/10/politics/republican-debate-marco-rubio-welders-philosophers/index.html.

4   Bureau of Labor Statistics, US Department of Labor, "Occupational Outlook Handbook: Welders, Cutters, Solderers, and Braziers," accessed January 10, 2022, https://www.bls.gov/ooh/production/welders-cutters-solderers-and-brazers.htm.

to work as philosophers (58 percent go on to graduate school).[5] They become college professors, lawyers, judges, and software developers, among hundreds of other professions. Even Google recruits philosophy majors because they often make excellent programmers—after all, computers are run by formal rules of logic, analogous to those taught in philosophy.

There are also passionate advocates for the humanities. Some believe that scholarship is an intrinsic benefit, an end in itself, that need not be extrinsically justified by social or economic benefits. Others believe we need to transmit our culture and values from one generation to another. They also contend that philosophy and many other liberal arts programs teach us to understand others, evaluate information, conduct research, and summarize complex material. They argue that walking a mile in the shoes of others, by reading their novels and studying their history and culture, makes better nurses, engineers, customer service representatives, managers, and citizens because they are likely to have more empathy for patients, customers, employees, and neighbors. As a history major, I am inclined to believe these claims. Unfortunately, it is difficult to prove or disprove them because the data on student participation in the humanities and its impact on adult behavior is missing or confounded.

In practice, we need well-trained professionals in hundreds of fields. We need electrical, chemical, and structural engineers. We need doctors, surgeons, and psychiatrists. We need software developers, computer engineers, and data scientists. And we also need auto technicians and welders. We need to teach grade school students, rear children, write news stories, run towns and states, and lead companies. We also need decent human beings, whether they are

---

5   Gray Associates analysis of the Public Use Microdata Sample (PUMS) of the American Community Survey (ACS) 2015–2019, United States Census Bureau.

engineers, philosophers, or welders. Accomplishing these goals will require both general humanities education and career training.

Personal aptitudes and preferences must be taken into account. Driving history majors, like me, into STEM fields may lead to more STEM graduates. It could also lead to more dropouts and bad engineers. Personally, I am certain that you would not want to ride in an elevator or drive across a bridge that I engineered. Some engineers might feel the same way about writing contracts or teaching in grade school. These diverse societal needs and personal aptitudes also pose the fundamental question: What should we teach?

Despite the importance and urgency of this question, academic program evaluations vary widely. At their worst, inertia, institutional politics, and loud voices dictate funding for current programs and new program launches. Faculty lines are viewed as sinecures, not strategic investments. Board members demand cuts using simplistic metrics, like the number of annual graduates from a program. Chancellors take unilateral action to control costs. New programs are launched with great aspirations and thin data, leading to costly failures that bleed money for years.

After more than a decade of work, our clients have taught us a great deal about how to evaluate programs. Our understanding and systems development have evolved through occasional flashes of insight and years of trial and error—bumping into gaps in data sets, finding important information missing, and discovering that existing "data" was often a myth or bad math.

Let's discuss an example. When we first began this work, clients asked us to analyze individual academic programs: Should we launch a bachelor of science in accounting? A critical piece of this analysis was an estimate of the number of jobs that would be available for accounting graduates. If accounting majors only became accountants and stayed accountants, this would be a simple piece of research. Empirically, most accounting graduates do go into accounting, but others go into finance and management, and a few become CEOs. To map graduates to jobs, we needed what is called a crosswalk between academic programs and jobs. As was the norm, we used the National Center for Education Statistics (NCES) crosswalk between programs and occupations. For example, we included all finance jobs as opportunities for accountants. I suspect most program analysts still use this one-program-at-a-time approach to calculate the number of jobs available for graduates.

It is flawed. We found the error when a client first asked us to analyze dozens of programs at a time so that they could understand all their options. One night, we loaded up a stack of cloud servers and used the NCES crosswalks to plow through all 700 Standard Occupational Classification codes, 1,400 academic programs, 6 degree levels, and a few hundred cities.

By the morning, our analysis had more than doubled the number of jobs in the US. It turns out that accounting graduates are not the only people who become finance managers. Business, finance, and even history majors do, too. Our one-at-a-time method assigned all one hundred finance jobs to accounting, then assigned them again to business graduates, and again to finance, and so forth, creating hundreds of "finance jobs" out of thin air.

To avoid double-counting, crosswalks must *allocate* jobs among all the programs that compete for positions in each occupation. Since then, we have spent years developing and refining a crosswalk that provides a more accurate, single-counted estimate of jobs by major. This crosswalk is a cornerstone of our program analyses.

Vital decisions on which programs to start, stop, or grow must be founded on reliable data. Obtaining reliable data takes time and money. Correctly analyzing it requires quite a bit of know-how. More specifically, solid program decisions require data on four topics:

1. *Mission:* Does the program support the institutional mission?

2. *Academic standards:* Is the program consistent with accreditor requirements and institutional expectations for student inclusion, retention, learning, and graduate outcomes?

3. *Markets:* Is the external environment for the program healthy? Do students seek it out? Will there be meaningful jobs and living wages for graduates? Is competition manageable?

4. *Margins:* Will the program consume financial resources or generate them?

While valid data is critical, program evaluation should be *data-informed*, not *data-driven*. There is no data or algorithm that can tell you what academic programs to offer. We suggest bringing the data to a broad cross section of the college community, including faculty and administrators, in a well-facilitated workshop that informs their judgment. It is a substantial investment of time that enables institutions to make better decisions about what programs to launch and grow and difficult decisions on programs to sunset. Importantly, the process strengthens campus relationships and develops a shared understanding of academic priorities. It avoids the rancor and campus rebellions that often follow top-down decisions. Most importantly, it leads to better decisions that strengthen relationships, reduce costs, and create new revenue streams that will sustain the institution for years to come.

> Vital decisions on which programs to start, stop, or grow must be founded on reliable data.

Skeptics may not believe these results are possible. There are widespread stereotypes about higher education: Institutions are slow to change, they endlessly debate options, and they are uninterested in facts about markets and financials. Our experience suggests that these stereotypes need not be true. When given appropriate, credible data and the opportunity to work with it, faculty and administrators usually arrive at sound decisions at least as quickly as many of the corporations I worked with before founding Gray Associates.

For colleges that are struggling financially, please do not delay this work. Once financial trouble starts, time is against you. Your options will be fewer and worse as the situation deteriorates. With enough lead time (eighteen to thirty-six months), launching new programs and investing to grow current programs can restore growth and income. Improving curricular efficiency can produce millions of dollars in savings in twelve to eighteen months. Once you are within a year of insolvency, there is little you can do.

For all schools, please do not make these decisions in a secret, top-down process. It may seem faster and safer, but it is not. Once announced, top-down decisions often elicit a storm of resistance, which delays implementation. Unions will immediately start to protect their members and block action. Someone will complain to the press, which can affect student recruiting and reduce enrollment, making financial problems worse. Top-down decisions may breach the principles of shared governance, which could lead to accreditation issues. Perhaps most importantly, top-down decisions are more likely to be wrong. You need input from experts in your disciplines and markets to make sound decisions. On a related note, a consultant's program recommendations usually face the same issues as top-down decisions. A consultant can provide data and facilitate the evaluation process, but your team should make the decisions.

It is worth investing the time and money to make better-informed program decisions. They can transform the institution and restore or strengthen its financial health. They can help your students succeed and support economic growth in your community.

Making the right program decisions is the cornerstone of academic program evaluation and management; however, even the best-designed portfolios need to be reviewed and managed much more frequently than every three to five years, which is the norm. Student demand ebbs and flows; whole new industries can emerge in a few years, competition is quick to saturate attractive programs, and your program economics can take a turn, for better or worse, in a few months. Academic leaders need to ask the right questions in frequent and reasonably formal program reviews—and they should expect program managers to have the data to answer them.

This book is intended to help you make better-informed program decisions and to better manage your academic program portfolio. It will describe the data you need and how to organize it. It will propose a process that brings together faculty and administrators and teaches them how to use the data to inform their judgment, make sound decisions, and better manage their programs. It will prepare you to do the work yourself or find outside help that has valid data, effective software, and proven processes for making and managing program decisions. It will prepare you to better answer the question: What programs should we start, stop, or grow?

CHAPTER 1

Academic Program Evaluation: Overview

Dr. Sue McDonald, college president, was sitting at her fifteen-foot conference table with legs of carved lion heads and claw feet. She loved the fierce antique carvings and recalled when Dr. Phillip Johnson, an art history professor, told her, "It is called a monopodium—a reproduction of an ancient Roman table leg." She wished the lions could protect Phil and her gifted professors.

The tone of conversations had changed since Phil and other deans had argued and laughed around the table beneath the windows that looked over the courtyard of brick paths, new grass, and blooming daffodils. Enrollment declines had ripped through budgets while heated discussions erupted among faculty, deans, and administrators trying to protect their departments and their livelihoods.

Sue looked up from her budget spreadsheets to greet Dr. Amy Smith, a new faculty member. Within a minute, Amy launched into a plea for a new European history program. "It could give our students a more global perspective and help them understand that Europe is a real place, with real people, that there is a world beyond Kansas. It could attract the top of the class from local high schools and strengthen our partnership with Ghent University in Belgium. Students gave it a 4.5 rating on my survey—they really are interested." Sue admired her for making the case for the program and wondered if Amy would survive the coming expense cuts. "Probably not," Sue thought. "Too new."

Amy pushed an article from the *Kansas Times* across the table and continued. "But that's not the most exciting news. Global Airlines is going to break ground on a headquarters building. They'll need people with an international perspective."

Sue recalled two boys in the dining hall who bragged that they had never gone to Missouri, just over the river from the campus. They did need perspective but were unlikely to enroll in a major about Missouri or Europe. Sue sighed. What a shame the college was going to lose such a talented, enthusiastic global thinker.

Shortly after Amy finished, John Axelrod, a local business-person and board member, lit up Sue's monitor. "Good morning, Sue. I booked this time to remind you about computational biology. There are jobs for computational biologists. The Bureau of Labor Statistics (BLS) says this is one of the fastest-growing fields in the US, and it's important to the community and the local economy. In fact, my company needs a couple of these scientists." Sue nodded; it might be an exciting field, though it was a little outside of the mission of a liberal arts university.

Sue considered the program proposals. Amy's small survey of an unrepresentative sample of students was weak evidence of demand for a European history program. Global was more likely to hire business graduates than history graduates. Axelrod's proposal was no better; he just wanted the university to absorb his training costs. She knew that Bureau of Labor Statistics forecasts were inaccurate, and Axelrod was quoting national estimates, which had little relevance in her market. In any case, his company couldn't hire the number of graduates needed to sustain a viable program, and he was unlikely to fund the replacement of the university's decrepit bio labs. Nonetheless, she was sure he would push for a board discussion of the program.

"These ideas are not going to help the budget or Amy," Sue thought. "I need a way to find programs that are consistent with our mission and that can improve our financials."

D r. McDonald faces a common set of issues: a budget shortfall, pressure to cut existing programs, passionate advocates for new programs, and no money available to fund them. Across higher education, program cuts are increasingly common and inflammatory. This situation requires a more informed, effective, and frequent approach to program evaluation.

Program evaluation is often confounded with program assessment. Program assessment should deeply explore the academic content of a program and generate goals and plans for improvement. It takes time and faculty participation. It must keep pace with the evolution of the discipline. In most cases, assessments need to be done every three to five years. Program evaluation should determine whether the program is viable and important to the institution. Faculty should be involved, as should managers in marketing, admissions, and other departments. Evaluations determine which programs to start, stop, or grow. Evaluations need to keep up with changes in external markets and internal economics, so they must be completed at least once a year.

Our clients tell us that their program evaluations are often poorly informed, sequential, opaque, and slow. Criteria and data required to evaluate programs are unclear. Recommendations are handed off from one person to another, but little information may be shared with the folks who made the recommendation. Over a year may pass before a recommendation is finally approved or denied. In the end, no one may be truly comfortable that the best decision was made. This slow, closed process invites suspicion and can lead to distrust in the institution and expensive mistakes that endure for years.

How do you evaluate programs in a thoughtful and well-informed way? It requires consistent criteria, sound data, and open discussion. A current or new program should further the institution's mission. It should deliver successful academic results. It should be in a healthy market, where student demand, employer needs, and competition are all attractive. While it may seem heretical, institutions must also analyze program economics, specifically margin.

Margin is important but not to earn a profit, pay dividends, or provide sinecures. Margin enables the institution to advance its mission. Programs with high margins may subsidize other programs and activities that are mission-critical. Margins may also pay for scholarships that improve access for low-income students and minorities. It's essential for academics to understand program margins so that they can craft a sustainable, inclusive program portfolio.

Briefly, successful program evaluations consider mission, academic performance, market attractiveness, and margins. They cover all program options, bringing together administration, faculty, and faculty union representatives (if any) to efficiently and openly reach decisions and strengthen relationships.

Mission

Accreditors require that every college or university have a mission statement. It is a meticulously crafted statement that speaks to stakeholders in a timeless style. As a result, as Robert Dickeson points out in *Prioritizing Academic Programs and Services: Reallocating Resources to Achieve Strategic Balance*, the institutional mission, by itself, is too broad to inform program decisions.

We suggest that colleges and universities deconstruct their mission into more specific attributes that are useful in evaluating programs. You may wish to address the fields of study the college should focus on, the types of students your college should serve, the educational outcomes you would like them to achieve, the life and work they should be prepared for after graduation, or the impact of the college on the local community.

Once you have deconstructed the mission statement, faculty can draft qualitative assessments of the fit of each program with the attributes of the mission. There is value in quantitative measures of mission fit—putting numbers to mission fit will help sustain its importance in the face of more easily quantified metrics. Simple ratings are all that's needed: mission-critical (about 10 percent of programs), mission-aligned (about 80 percent of programs), and discretionary (about 10 percent of programs that are not closely related to the mission).

However, going beyond qualitative assessments and quantifying the mission is surprisingly contentious. Every program has its advocates, who may fear low scores. Others may see quantifying mission-fit as reductionist and meaningless because the concepts involved are complex and ill-defined. Assigning a number to mission is not essential. You may want to test the waters with a few professors and deans to see how controversial it may be before you attempt it.

While some may see the work as a veiled threat, the goal is to identify and defend mission-critical programs when other numeric data is unfavorable.

Academic Standards

The evaluation of the academic quality of a program should be distinguished from an academic assessment. Let's break the evaluation of academic standards into three broad categories: inputs, instruction, and outcomes.

For *inputs*, you may wish to consider whether the program can attract the quantity, type, and quality of students and faculty the college seeks. For *instruction*, student progress is a critical factor that includes metrics like course completion and graduation rates. *Outcomes* may include going to graduate school, getting a job, and wages. An illustration of high-level academic program evaluation metrics follows. Note that it allows the data to be filtered by student segments, including ethnicity and income.

SELECT TO FILTER COURSE DEPARTMENT ▼

CATEGORY	METRIC	2020	2021	CHANGE
Program Profile	# of Students	203	197	-3%
	# of SCH Taught	5,439	4,730	-13%
	% SCH in Online Courses	7%	9%	22%
	% SCH Taught by FT Faculty	57%	57%	0%
	% SCH Taught by Tenure/Track	55%	55%	0%
Department Profile	# of Full-Time Faculty	11	17	32%
	# of Part-Time Faculty	49	70	28%
	% SCH Taught In-Dept	23%	24%	2%
Student Progress	# Students Enrolled 2+ Terms	159	139	-8%
	# Students Return from Prior Yr.	137	131	-3%
	# Students Enrolled 15+ CH	202	188	-7%
	% Students Complete 15+ CH	62%	65%	3%
	Withdraw/D/F Rate	27%	24%	-11%
Outcomes	# of Completions	28	45	38%
	Median Time to Complete (Yrs)	3.10	3.20	3%
	Benchmark Exam/ Licensure Pass Rate	83%	87%	4%
	Avg. End-of-Program Survey Rating	77%	80%	3%

Pell Status		Age Group		Gender		Race/Ethnicity							
Non	Pell	<25	25+	M	F	White	Lat/His	Asian	UNKN	Black	Ntv Am	2+	Interntl

Outcomes, particularly employment and wages, are all the rage in program evaluation. States are creating incentive funding to drive outcomes, especially completion by underserved and minority students. In other cases, they provide differential funding for STEM programs, because employers need these graduates.

These incentives may generate unexpected consequences. They may promote tighter admissions standards rather than better teaching. A focus on STEM may tend to exclude underserved minorities and Pell Grant recipients. Nonetheless, healthy programs produce graduates, not just credit hours. Students should leave prepared for life, employment, or graduate school. They should be able to earn a wage that justifies their investment in higher education. All these outcomes can now be tracked and should be considered in program evaluation.

Now let's turn from academic standards to evaluating markets for academic programs.

The Four Dimensions of Program Market Evaluation

Over a decade ago, Universal Technical Institute was one of our first clients. Their CEO, Kim McWaters, set out a strategy that created a competitive advantage for her institution and led to solid jobs for her graduates. The strategy tightly linked the institute to the few large employers, like GM and Toyota, that dominated the auto industry and its dealers. Linking her brand to the employers strengthened its appeal to prospective students. Employers helped fund and equip classrooms. The relationship with employers ensured that more than 90 percent of graduates won jobs in fields related to their training after graduation and, in many cases, before it. Naturally, this led us to focus on *employer demand* as the primary criterion in our early program evaluations.

This approach worked for Universal Technical Institute, though it is a bit myopic for other institutions. In Kim's case, for decades there was a fairly steady supply of students interested in becoming auto technicians. For many other programs, the link between employer demand and student demand is weaker. Psychology is an enormous undergraduate program, one of the largest in the US. However, only 2 percent of psychology graduates will seek a career in a field for which they are directly prepared, 50 percent will go on to graduate school, and others will enter hundreds of fields that are loosely or not at all related to their degree. Should colleges close their psychology programs? Should they avoid large programs that don't prepare students for specific jobs? For many colleges, the answer is no, not if they want to survive.

To survive, colleges need to consider *student demand* in addition to employer demand. For the most part, students fill seats and pay tuition, not employers. Even in Kim's case, employers rarely paid for their students. This is not to say that employment is not important—it is. But students usually pay the bills. When finances matter, data on student demand is essential.

Like today's educational leaders, Kim was also concerned about *competition*. In most markets and programs, competition in higher education is intensifying, led by massive open online course (MOOC) providers, national online institutions, and increasingly aggressive local and regional colleges. So, when picking a program, it is best to see who's already

> When finances matter, data on student demand is essential.

out there and determine whether you can successfully compete against them or find a niche they missed.

Competition should not always be feared. One of our clients has opened several new campuses. Each of these campuses took 50 percent of the market away from the established institutions. The client offered a better program, recruited competitors' admissions representatives, and spent more on marketing. For this client, competition was food. For most colleges, it shows that there is a proven market for a program.

Last but not least, consider whether the program should be taught at a *degree level* you offer. A community college won't want to offer an associate's degree program in neurosurgery; a Tier 1 research institution should not offer a doctoral degree in carpentry. Filter out programs that don't fit the degree levels you offer or plan to offer.

There you have it, the four dimensions of academic program *market* evaluation: student demand, employment, competition, and degree level.

Margins

Good academic program decisions require more than market data; they also cry out for information on the financial margins that programs produce or consume. As mentioned previously, nonprofit colleges do not seek margin as an end in itself, nor should they. They exist to realize their mission, and realizing the mission requires funding. A healthy portfolio of academic programs can and usually should generate enough margin to sustain and invest in the mission.

From a financial perspective, what is a program? It is not just courses in a specific department. It is all the courses taken by the students in a major. It includes their general education courses and electives, many of which may be taught outside the department. As a result, most programs have long tentacles that affect the number of sections, instructors, and costs across the institution. Often, the high margins on general education courses help to offset the high-cost courses in technical and clinical programs. Of course, program margin includes the courses in the department, too. The averaging of high-margin and low-margin courses inside and outside the department allows most programs, even small ones, to be contribution positive.

Nonetheless, in a healthy portfolio, some programs may need financial help. If they are important to the mission, subsidizing these programs is appropriate. Making these investments purposefully requires hard data on the revenue, cost, and margin of all academic programs (as well as a clear-eyed view of each program's importance to the mission). With the data, you can make wise investments in programs that will grow and produce money; you can also gauge how much to spend on money-losing, mission-critical programs.

Importantly, neither market nor margin information alone is sufficient. Let's use the following illustration, which shows program margin on the vertical axis and market attractiveness on the horizontal axis. Two programs, A and B, have similar and low margins. Program A is in the lower-left corner; it has low margins in an unhealthy market. This one is hard to fix. Growth is unlikely, since the market is weak and the school does not yet know how to run it at a profit. It is not mission-critical, so this program is a questionable investment of resources. On the other hand, Program B has equally low margins, but it is in a healthy market, and it is mission-critical. With some added investment, it might be able to grow, generate margin, and contribute more substantially to the mission.

ACADEMIC PROGRAM PORTFOLIO EVALUATION VISUALIZATION

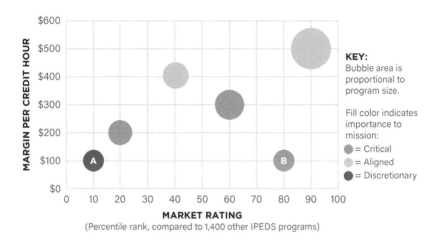

Integrated Program Evaluation

With data on markets and margins, program evaluation can begin. Program evaluation is a team sport. It is vital to involve the right people in an open, data-informed process. Involvement is especially important if the institution is in crisis. During a crisis, people justifiably fear for their jobs and their families. They are likely to assume the worst—that somewhere ill-informed, unfair decisions are being made for political reasons that are beyond their control. In the interests of speed, the president, the board, and others may, in fact, be making decisions. These top-down approaches often have poor results. They frequently lead to an uproar on campus and damaging stories in the news, both of which may hurt enrollment and revenue. Further, rules of shared governance, unions,

> Program evaluation is a team sport. It is vital to involve the right people in an open, data-informed process.

and other resistance often delay implementation by months or years. All this is avoidable by including the provost, the deans, selected faculty, and the heads of admissions, marketing, student services, and institutional research in a well-run, data-informed process that respects shared governance. In our experience, most people working in higher education, including faculty senate members or union leaders, are willing to make sound decisions, if provided the right data and a voice in the program portfolio evaluation process.

Program portfolio evaluation is not a one-time event. You will also need the tools, time, and processes to review each program far more frequently than is the norm today. You will need ongoing reports on market trends, competition, enrollment, and student success. You should review some of these metrics quarterly, others annually. Deep dives into the content of programs (assessment) can be less frequent, but in fast-moving fields like computer science, they may need to be done annually rather than every five years.

Later chapters will describe how to get and use data on markets and margins to make better-informed program decisions. The analysis will not make the decisions for you, but it will increase the odds of making the right program decisions and improving the financial health and educational quality of your institution.

As a faculty member, Sue had seen program edicts that made little sense academically or financially. She had watched deans wait until critics were away from the Provosts' Council meeting to gain approval for new programs. In one case, her whole group was moved to another department in exchange for a dean's support for a flagging program. She smiled as she recalled a faculty member who asked for more time for a program to prove itself, though it had only one graduate a year. One of his peers asked how long the program had been offered. The professor confessed that it had been on the books for a decade.

Sue thought, "We need a better process and much better data. We need to listen to employers and be sure we can attract enough students to pay the bills. We complain that the number of high school students is declining while underserving online opportunities and the adults in our community who need new skills. The competition will be intense, but we should be able to win on our home turf, where people like us and have known us for one hundred years. With support from the faculty and administration, we can turn this around. First things first. Let's define our market so that we can pull data for it."

CHAPTER 2

Defining Your Market

When Sue began talking with her team about market analysis, she quickly realized that everyone had a different definition of the school's market. The director of athletics pointed out that the college recruited athletes from across the country. The director of adult and online learning agreed that the college served the entire US market and some overseas students. Admissions and marketing said that most students, even online students, came from within seventy miles of the campus. Sue was a little frustrated that the college did not have a clear answer to a basic question. She also suspected that there might not be one answer—the college might serve several markets.

The first step in market analysis is to correctly define the markets to be analyzed. This work ensures that your data includes relevant prospects, employers, and competitors. It answers two questions: Where do our current students come from? Where are the other students we aspire to reach? Just a few years ago, these were difficult questions to answer. Geographic analysis, drive time, and distance calculations required esoteric software that few people could use. These days, determining geographic markets served is fairly easy.

The first step is to pull students' home addresses. The college may have several addresses on file for each student. For example, you may have a current home address and the student's school year address in off-campus housing. The best address for this analysis is the home address, sometimes called the permanent address, that the student used when applying to college. This address is in the market that your students originally came from.

When we do the work, we use mapping software to geocode the student addresses into census tracts. We use tracts for several reasons. Their geographic boundaries are well known, they are included in many mapping applications, and the shape files are free to download. They are highly detailed. There are 73,057 tracts in the US, and on average, each one has four thousand people. Census tracts align precisely with state borders and census data on population and demographics.

You may use zip codes instead. There are 41,702 zip codes, so they are 43 percent less detailed than census tracts. Zip codes do not align neatly with state boundaries and census data. They do have a virtue—they do not require use of any personally identifiable information, such as student addresses. Larger geographic units, such as counties and cities, are usually too big to be useful in determining the market you serve. They may stretch for dozens of miles and over an hour of drive time.

At this point, you'll have counts of students by tract or zip. The next step is to calculate the distance from your campus to every tract or zip in your data. Then you can add up students by distance from campus. We find it helpful to create a chart like the following one that shows the cumulative percentage of students by distance from campus. In this case, about 90 percent of students come from within twenty-five miles of campus.

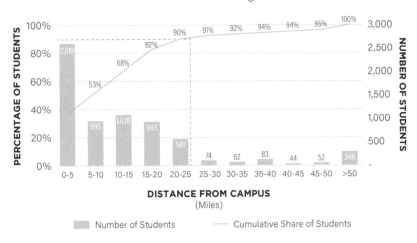

DISTRIBUTION OF STUDENTS BY DISTANCE FROM CAMPUS
Small Public College

Source; Three years of enrollment data for approximately 7,000 first-time students. Excludes international students.

It may also be helpful to create heat maps that show where your students are concentrated. In many cases, you will find that most students come from less than one hundred miles from campus. Interestingly, even online students tend to cluster close to campus, though some will be farther away.

If your students commute to campus, you may want to analyze drive time to campus from each tract. It is a more complex and slower calculation, but a few hours of calculation time will give commuter campuses in high-traffic areas (e.g., Los Angeles) a more accurate market definition. The results are similar to distance analysis and will show the volume of students by drive time.

If student addresses are not easily available, there is an alternative or complementary analysis. Almost all students looking for college will use Google at some point in their search. Working with your marketing department or directly in Google AdWords, you can get counts of Google searches for your brand name by zip code. This, too, can be charted and mapped to illustrate where students who consider your college are located. Brand search is a complement to the student analysis, since it may show how broadly your brand is considered *before* students contact the college. You may find that there is a broader market in which you are considered than there is for your actual students. Be careful to use search terms that are unique to your brand. Arizona State University will only count folks who searched for the University, but "ASU" will pick up searches for Arizona State University and for Alabama State University.

For some colleges, the definition of markets is more complex. I remember a religious school whose students came from pockets spread across the nation. In this case, it made sense to find the areas where members of the church tended to cluster. These areas could then be grouped into one "market." For online programs, broader market definitions may also make sense, even if they are aspirational. In most cases, at Gray Associates, we use the local market, the regional market, and the national market for online. It is also worth exploring whether definitions should vary by academic program. Some programs will attract commuting and residential students from quite a distance. Nursing is a good example. Seats in nursing programs are constrained by clinical sites and state boards of nursing; as a result, interested students will travel farther to find a school that will accept them. Other programs, like medical assisting, often draw most of their students from an area less than ten miles around the campus.

While you may not evaluate international as a separate market, it can be an important group of potential students. In some programs, like master's degrees in computer science, the majority of students in the US come from overseas (I suspect US students with computer science skills are too busy making money to go to graduate school). These students could be full-paying students in your programs, so we suggest including data on international demand to supplement your local or US data.

Finally, there is no need to rely on just one market definition. You may need one for your campus-based programs, another for online, and still another for graduate programs. This does imply more work pulling data for each of several market definitions, but once the work is done, it is fairly straightforward to use one definition for one set of questions or programs and a different one for others.

Displaying Your Data

Once you have gathered all the numbers, you are almost ready to evaluate them. However, you may be looking at numbers and trends you have never seen before, making the interpretation of the data challenging. Are five thousand Google searches for a program in New York a lot? How accurate are BLS forecasts? Is 2 percent growth in jobs in a Standard Occupational Classification code exciting, or should it make you yawn and move on to the next program?

This was abruptly brought home to me by a board member who was discussing a program with us. It was quite some time ago, when we had just found a source for inquiries that provides timely data on student demand by program. During the discussion, I was proud to point out that we now had thousands of local inquiries for the program. She asked, "Is that a lot?" I sat quietly. I knew there were thousands, but I did not know how the number compared to other programs and markets.

After this unpleasant experience, I tried to find a way to put our numbers into context and make them easier to interpret. To provide context, we have settled on two complementary approaches: percentiles and internal benchmarks. If you gather data on a wide range of programs, or all fourteen hundred Integrated Postsecondary Education Data System (IPEDS) programs, it is helpful to calculate their percentile rank on each metric. The program I discussed with the board member was in the 98th percentile for inquiries, so I could have known that student demand for the program was unusually high and saved myself some embarrassment.

While you may not have time to collect data on all IPEDS programs, you should collect data on all the programs offered by your university. In this case, the percentiles would show how one of your programs compared to all your others. An even simpler method is to select a program you currently offer as a benchmark. For the benchmark, we suggest using a program that you know well, appears to be healthy, and has five or more years of history. The benchmark will provide a reasonable comparison with other programs that are less familiar to you, especially potential new programs.

To make the data easier to interpret, we suggest color-coding the percentiles. Programs are not inherently bad or good but can be attractive or unattractive based on strategic and market fit for your institution. The color coding allows you to grasp that quickly. We use a simple green, blue, yellow, and red color scale, with green being best and red being worst. This variation on traffic light colors is intuitive for people to understand (remember to include the numbers, too, for people who cannot distinguish red and green). Now, when your team looks at the data and sees a lot of green, they will know immediately that they are looking at a promising program and can quickly identify any weaknesses that are shown in red.

Consistency in the presentation of the data will also help people understand it more quickly. Try to create a format for your program data that is logical and easy to maintain. The format should reinforce the categories of data (e.g., student demand, employment, competition, and degree fit) so that they become accepted as the right topics to consider. Then keep using the same format so that people become accustomed to it and can more easily draw valid comparisons and conclusions.

Similar to a student paper or a test, program evaluations should include a *scoring rubric*. The rubric should set thresholds for each metric and assign weights for achieving each threshold. The thresholds and weights should reflect what is important to your college. Some clients heavily weight jobs, because preparing students for work is a central part of their mission. Others more heavily weight student demand to ensure that classes are filled and budgets are met. For some, intense competition may receive heavy negative weights while others view it as an opportunity to take share and assign it positive weights. In most cases, colleges tend to equally weight employment and student demand and give a lower weight to competition. Degree level is usually assigned negative weights if the program does not fit the degree levels offered by the college.

The *scoring process* is important, too. To create the initial scoring rubric, start with a small group that has a strong appetite for detail and numbers,

However, our experience suggests that groups are more likely to trust and use scoring systems they have helped to create.

since scoring involves dozens of metrics, thresholds, and weights. However, our experience suggests that groups are more likely to trust and use scoring systems they have helped to create. Once the small group has drafted the rubric, we suggest that a larger, more representative group discuss and refine the scoring, often at the category level (e.g., student demand vs. employment). The discussion helps to clarify institutional priorities and the goals of program evaluation. It usually leads to some changes in the initial rubric and broader acceptance of the rubric itself. Perhaps most important, it provides a reasonably objective and transparent score and rank for current and potential new programs, which will prove helpful in managing the politics of program evaluation.

Market definition went well and quickly, to Sue's surprise. Student home addresses were easy to pull. Institutional research ran a distance analysis and created a histogram that illustrated the percentage of the college's students by their distance from the campus. The cabinet seemed genuinely interested in the data. Overall, 80 percent of students came from within sixty miles; the cabinet agreed that this was a reasonable core market. Online stretched a little farther, but eighty miles captured almost all online students. The rest of the college's students were scattered across the country, most likely the result of athletic recruiting, and the cabinet agreed to add a national market definition to the local and online market definitions. It was all over in less than an hour.

She mulled over how the program evaluations would go.

The deans had already begun lobbying for their programs. The head of the faculty union had promised to oppose any program cuts while finance was pushing for a 10 percent reduction in academic cost. A few years ago, President Frei- berger tried to clean up this mess, and it cost him his job.

It was going to be a wild ride.

CHAPTER 3

Understanding Student Demand

The spring sun streamed through the large leaded windows in Sue's office as she reviewed the results for a technology program the college had launched in the fall. It had attracted only a handful of students, most of whom had switched from a related major. Expensive new labs and high-tech classrooms were sitting empty.

She knew it was an important field. The state had targeted the field for investment, and several large local employers were willing to offer internships and pay top dollar for program graduates. But students did not seem to know about the program, or they simply were not interested in it. She wondered what she should have done to avoid such an expensive mistake.

To better understand what went wrong, Sue organized a postmortem.

Marketing washed its hands of the program. "No one asked us to provide data on search volumes before the launch. As you can see, they are a fraction of what we need for a successful program."

Admissions followed suit. "Very few candidates qualify for the program. When they do, they usually go down the street where they have one of the best programs in the state and can offer more financial aid."

Sue asked about the survey that said 20 percent of students were interested in the program. A new faculty member spoke up. "Actually, the survey was correct. We surveyed students in the department, and 20 percent said they were interested. That is consistent with the number of students in the department who changed majors to enroll in the new program."

"Almost all the students in the new program came from an existing program?" Sue asked.

The faculty member responded, "Uh ... yes, I guess. But they might have gone to a different college if we did not offer it."

Over the last few decades, measuring student demand has become more complex. Student demand is no longer equal to the number of upcoming and recent graduates from local high schools. Over the last twenty years, many adults have decided to start college while others returned to college to complete degrees. More recently, thousands of adults began going to coding boot camps, getting certificates, or learning skills in nondegree online courses from colleges located thousands of miles away from home, and hundreds of thousands of international students attend American universities every year. Student demand has broken into segments, including age, race, gender, income, academic aptitude, location, country of origin, and others.

For program evaluation, the critical segmentation is by program of interest. The goal is to estimate how many potential students are interested in programs that you offer or new programs that you could develop. It should also distinguish between student demand for on-campus and online programs.

Student demand data helps institutions answer several questions:

- How big is the opportunity for this program?
- Is the opportunity growing?
- Is the opportunity primarily online or on-campus?
- What is my market share? Is it growing?
- Is this program likely to generate margin?

Programs with strong student demand usually generate higher margins. As illustrated here, student demand explains about 50 percent of the variation in program margins. For schools facing financial challenges, this is a vital concept. Within reason, they should focus on programs that have strong and growing student demand, as these are the programs that can generate the revenue and margins needed to improve an institution's financial health.

> Programs with strong student demand usually generate higher margins.

PROGRAM CONTRIBUTION VS. STUDENT DEMAND SCORE

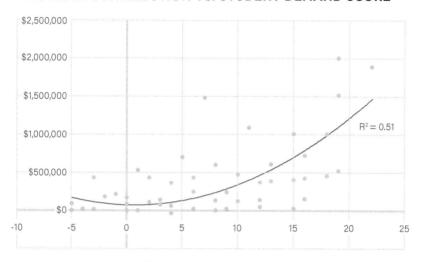

STUDENT DEMAND SCORE

PROGRAM CONTRIBUTION:
PREDICTIVE VALUE (r²) OF MARKET METRICS

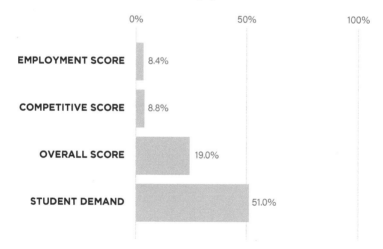

Student demand also distinguishes between small, high-potential programs and weaker ones. A small program in a market with healthy student demand may be an opportunity for growth. In contrast, a small program with weak and declining student demand is unlikely to grow and may be a candidate to sunset, especially if it is tangentially related to mission and has low or negative margins.

It is important to distinguish fads from programs with rapid, sustainable growth. In the early 2000s, the television series *CSI: Crime Scene Investigation* drew thousands of college students into crime scene investigator programs (only to find that there were almost no jobs available after graduation). More recently, during the pandemic, interest in public health programs grew rapidly, but they may decline as the pandemic subsides. Student interest in data science and cybersecurity are exploding; I believe this is probably not a fad and is more likely the start of two long-term trends.

Some drivers of student demand are unreliable. Legislation and regulation can create extrinsically motivated student demand with the stroke of a pen. As an example, some states pay more to teachers with a master's degree, which usually leads to full classes in master's programs in education. Unfortunately, a change in legislation can also destroy a program in an instant. One of our clients had a thriving master's program in education until the state incentive was withdrawn and the program shrank to nothing.

Intrinsic student interest in a subject such as psychology is likely to be more sustained. Fundamental technology trends, such as cyber risk and the declining cost and increasing power of semiconductors, are also likely to endure. Demographic trends typically take decades to play out, and their end can usually be foreseen well in advance, giving an institution time to adapt. Even legislation may last, if it rests on a solid base of public support, like Social Security, Medicare, Medicaid, and, perhaps, the Affordable Care Act.

Discovering Student Demand Data

The data sources on student demand range from comprehensive, slow-moving federal data sets to up-to-the-minute snapshots for popular programs. The most comprehensive source is IPEDS. This system is run by the US Department of Education; every school that accepts Title IV funding (federal financial aid) must file completions by program once a year. IPEDS completions include all students, online or on-campus, who complete a program or certificate at a Title IV institution. The data goes back for decades and covers roughly 1,400 programs offered by over 4,000 institutions. It includes information on gender and ethnicity by program and institution.

IPEDS groups programs into CIP codes (Classification of Instructional Programs). In 2012 and again in 2020, IPEDS made changes to its CIP code taxonomy; for example, data science will now have its own CIP. The changes will make it somewhat more difficult to track the history and long-term trends for these programs. While I will deal with employer demand in the next chapter, it is worth noting here that CIP codes are not the same as Standard Occupational Classification codes (SOCs). As a result, complex mapping must be done to estimate which SOCs and jobs align with a given CIP and its graduates; these crosswalks must be updated with the new CIP codes.

Like every large data set, IPEDS has limitations. The information on students' program choices is dated. As I write this, the most current release came out two years ago. Students choose their major two or more years before graduating, so the information on what students want is four or more years out of date. In a few months, the update for last year's graduates will be published, which will represent decisions made three or more years ago.

Completing the IPEDS data filings is a large and tedious project for each college. Program filings can be made in over 1,400 CIP codes and a half dozen degree levels, leaving many opportunities for error. For example, one auto mechanic training school files its graduates under the CIP for auto engineering, so we correct the mistake in our data sets. When pulling data for your analyses, you may wish to pull all the related programs as well so that you can correct obvious errors made by your primary competitors.

Completions for online programs are usually reported to the physical main campus of the institution—not the markets in which students are actually located. In 2019, approximately twenty-nine thousand completions for the University of Phoenix showed up in Phoenix, even though over 95 percent of these students never set foot in Arizona.[6] This reporting skews the results in both the main campus's market and everywhere else. In Phoenix, programs appear saturated by the twenty-nine thousand reported completions. In Southern California, the data suggests that there is little online activity, despite thousands of students attending online programs offered by institutions from Phoenix, including Grand Canyon University, Arizona State University, and the University of Phoenix.

To correctly estimate online completions by market, my team uses data from the National Council for State Authorization Reciprocity Agreements (NC-SARA). NC-SARA is a nonprofit organization that covers thousands of institutions in forty-nine member states, the District of Columbia, Puerto Rico, and the US Virgin Islands. California has not and probably will not join NC-SARA (the legislature believes that joining NC-SARA will encourage for-profit institutions to enter California). Institutions register once and

---

6   US Department of Education, National Center for Education Statistics, "Integrated Postsecondary Education Data System (IPEDS), 2010–2020 Completions," accessed January 10, 2022, https://nces.ed.gov/ipeds/use-the-data; National Council for State Authorization of Reciprocity Agreements, accessed January 10, 2022, https://nc-sara.org/.

are then able to offer their programs in all of the member states. The institutions must report online enrollment by state but not by program. You can use the NC-SARA data to reallocate enrollment back to the states in which students are physically located. You then need to use other data to estimate enrollment by program and to assign it to local markets within each state.

The allocation of online students into local markets seemed simple enough—that is, until we got started. Gray Associates had to run calculations for over 2,000 schools, 1,400 programs, 6 degree-levels, 50 states, and 74,000 local census tracts. This work tied up an analyst for several months and one of our high-speed workstations for days.

Even without these substantial corrections, IPEDS can give an institution a strong sense of the normal size of a program. In addition, a college can roughly estimate how big its current or new programs should be, using IPEDS completions for its peers. IPEDS also reveals on-campus competition and market share by program and location. In addition to completions by program, IPEDS includes a great deal of useful information, including overall enrollment, completion rates, and dozens of other data sets for both online and on-campus institutions.

Google Trends and AdWords

There are other sources of data on student demand that are more current, more local, and part of students' normal college search process. The first is Google, including the Google Keyword Planner. Using Keyword Planner, you can find the most common search terms and search volumes for each program you wish to explore. Unfortunately, your research must be done one program at a time, as we found out when Keyword Planner shut down our automated data pulls. It also requires setting up an account and giving it a credit card, although you do not have to pay for any ads. The estimated search volumes tend to be reported in large buckets (e.g., ten thousand to one hundred thousand searches per month), which is not useful for fine-grained analysis but could distinguish duds from stars.

Google Trends is a free index of search volumes for a given keyword or phrase and is a practical way to quickly check a potential program's size and growth. Pick a program-related word or phrase that a prospective student might search for, enter it, and you can see search trends going back to 2004 by metro area. Each data point is indexed to the maximum value for the time period and location you select, so you can see trends by season and over time but not the actual volume of searches. As a result, the Google Trends index for "Ugaritic programs" will peak at one hundred and so will the Trends index for "MBA programs," though MBA programs have many more students.

To make the data more useful, pick an existing program that you know well and run keywords for the existing and new program through Google Trends at the same time. If it shows the new program's index is two times the index for your current program, then search volume for the new program is double the demand for your current program—a good indicator of potential program size.

Using the right keywords, search volumes can be collected for specific markets and by degree level. For example, keywords could be tailored to a master's degree in nursing in Minneapolis and correctly distinguish it from the interest in a bachelor's degree in nursing in Chicago.

Terms that are ambiguous will cast a wider net than you intended. As mentioned earlier, the keyword "ASU" returns searches for Arizona State University and Alabama State University. To check, just enter your term into a browser; if the results are broader than you intended, try to find another keyword. You should also test various keywords to be sure you pick the best ones for a program or you may underestimate student demand.

There are easier ways. Your marketing department or agency can usually pull Google search volumes. Chances are they have search volumes for current programs and can get them for new programs. If that fails, you can subscribe to a service that tracks keyword searches. Or you are welcome to subscribe to Gray's systems, which include keyword search volume and trends by program and geographic market (down to the census tract).

Inquiries

There is a third source for data on student demand: inquiry aggregators and marketing agencies. These intermediaries place ads for programs that attract potential students and capture student contact information and interests by program, degree level, location, and modality (online vs. on-campus). These inquiries are sold to colleges and universities. If you work with an aggregator or a related agency, they will usually share inquiry volumes by program. At Gray, we maintained over eighty million inquiries and received hundreds of thousands of new inquiries per month. While the data was robust, it was skewed by the kinds of programs or institutions that were willing to pay for inquiries, which were typically online and vocationally oriented institutions. As a result, inquiries skewed toward work-related programs and were thin for humanities. Inquiries may also be underrepresented in states that more tightly regulate higher education, particularly New York. Given the issues with this data, we have stopped collecting and reporting on inquiries.

Enrollment

The National Student Clearinghouse captures data on enrollment by program, degree level, modality, and student home addresses. Colleges submit the data three times a year, so it is reasonably current. It is also very complete and generally accurate, though it is subject to institutional reporting errors. The data is fairly expensive, so you may need to fall back on Google's free data.

International

Many programs are able to recruit students from around the world, so we suggest gathering data from an international aggregator such as Studyportals. They can provide data on student interest (page views) by program, country, and city of origin. This gives a sense of international demand, both by program and by location. If you do not have access to an aggregator, similar data can be pulled from Google for most countries, notably excluding China. Keep in mind that Google may not be the primary search provider in a country; for more accurate data, you may need to research search engine share by country and then go to the local providers to find their search volumes for US college programs.

Limitations of Programmatic Demand Indicators

All data on student inquiries or searches by program has a limitation. Many students focus their college search by institution, not by program; they may not choose their major until their sophomore year (or later). As a result, programmatic search volumes may understate interest in programs that students tend to pick once they are in college. It is also true that many students change their major before or after entering college.

Often you will find that inquiries, Google, and international sources provide conflicting data on program size and growth. In this situation, I usually rely on IPEDS for insights on program size since it covers all programs, and overall program size usually does not change rapidly. On the other hand, if the data on growth trends conflicts, I would rely on more current sources: Google Trends and Google AdWords. The National Student Clearinghouse is not quite as current as Google (since it reports on students after they have selected a college); however, it is a comprehensive source on recent enrollment trends and program size.

Less-Than-Degree Courses and Certificates

Interest in less-than-degree courses and certificates is much more difficult to track. IPEDS has some information on certificates, but it is grouped into CIP codes, which mask specific certificates and skills. In my opinion, the best indicator of student demand for certificates and skills is available on MOOC websites. Working with MOOCs, Gray has developed a data set on student demand for less-than-degree courses and skills training. We are also building a set of keywords for skills and certificates so that we can pull Google search volumes and related information on jobs and skills. These data sets will be the first of their kind.

Surveys

I am skeptical of surveys about student demand for academic programs. Response rates are usually under 1 percent, which may not accurately represent the population. As a result, the sample is often biased and small (e.g., one hundred currently-enrolled students). It is seldom large enough to accurately assess interest in one program, let alone all current or new programs. As in all surveys, students may respond with their intentions, aspirations, or social biases, which often differ from their behaviors. This would be acceptable if there were no better ways to assess student demand. But there are. All the sources described previously rely on huge volumes of data on *student behavior*, which is a more reliable predictor of students' program choices than a small, quickly outdated survey of students' *stated intentions*.

Surveys do have their place. Gray uses sophisticated surveys to optimize institutional pricing and value propositions. For existing or potential new programs, you may wish to assess how students perceive the program and what aspects of the program they particularly value. This data can enable you to differentiate, market, and recruit for the program more effectively.

Summary of Data Sources

In our experience, IPEDS, Google Trends, Google AdWords, the National Student Clearinghouse, and international pageviews are the best sources of data on student demand by program. For less-than-degree courses and certificates, MOOC offerings illustrate hotter topics. All of these sources reveal actual student search behaviors, the samples are massive, and the data can be kept up to date.

There may well be other sources; in particular, colleges may have access to data at NCES or the testing services. If you find a good source, please let us know. Gray is always on the hunt for more and better data on higher-education programs.

Applying the Data

Once you have the data in hand, you can begin evaluating current and potential new programs. First, look at the volume of student demand: How many completions, searches, or enrollments are there? How does the volume compare to successful programs at your college? At this point, most programs in the US are mature and are growing slowly or not at all. There may still be growth opportunities if they are big enough for you to attract full cohorts of students or to increase attendance in your existing programs.

Other programs still have growing student demand. Trends are particularly important for new programs: It should be easier to carve out a niche in a growing market and quite challenging to grow in a declining market. Please be careful with programs that have extremely high percentage growth rates. When you find a program in IPEDS growing over 100 percent annually, chances are the program started out small and its numbers are still negligible. You may want to screen out programs whose numbers are inconsequential to avoid this issue. In other cases, reporting errors or changes move hundreds of students from one program to another within a discipline, which appears to be rapid growth or decline in the affected program. Double-check the data for the broader discipline (two- or four-digit CIP code), program, and institution before banking on fast changes in student demand. If one institution suddenly grows a program from zero to dozens of graduates, check to see if they recently acquired a school or changed the CIP in which they report the program's graduates.

Large programs may have low percentage growth rates, but the number of incremental completions may exceed the total number of completions in a smaller program. Keep track of unit growth (i.e., an increase in enrollment or the number of completions per year) to identify big programs with high unit growth but low percentage growth.

Sadly, student interest in many programs is declining. Some of this decline can be attributed to misinformation about career prospects for a given major or the humanities in general (more on this later). Nonetheless, with fewer students enrolled in a given program, you may need to pare back its electives and sections. While this is painful, it can free up resources to invest in growth areas, which in turn can generate the funds needed to keep smaller programs alive.

There is no need to do this work alone. Start with opportunities for growth. Invite your marketing and admissions teams to look at the data and discuss whether it aligns with their experience. Include deans and faculty who usually enjoy the search for promising programs. Emphasize that this is the first step in a process and that no decisions will be made on student demand alone. Teach your team to really look at the data to find opportunities and risks, instead of rehashing their favorite ideas. At this point, there is no need to wrangle over declining programs—that can usually wait until you have data on competition, employment, and economics.

In summary, student demand is one of the cornerstones of a healthy program portfolio and sustainable financials. It is a vital element in new program selection and an important gauge of the performance and market opportunity for existing programs. Good student demand data is accessible, inexpensive, or free. The best, fully curated data is

> Student demand is one of the cornerstones of a healthy program portfolio and sustainable financials.

not free, but it is vital—better to spend a little money to get the best data than to spend a lot of money launching the wrong program.

> Sue scanned the new program proposal on her desk. It started with ten pages on student demand, prepared by a team from the academic department, marketing, and admissions. It compared data for a successful current program with student demand data for the new program. The new program was clearly stronger—demand was higher and growing faster, not in one data source but in all of them. Admissions documented dozens of potential applicants who turned down the college because it did not offer the program. The dean pointed out that this program would not attract their traditional students because it required a vastly different set of skills.
>
> Sue thought, "It looks as though there is demand to fill enough seats to meaningfully increase enrollment. But will there be jobs for our graduates? How much would they be paid? Would it justify their investment in the degree?
>
> Next to the proposal was a request to replace a faculty member in a small program with declining enrollment. Sue wondered why the program was declining. "Is the market small? Is student demand trending down? Or can we fix it? I need the same data for this program that I have for the new program."

CHAPTER 4

Employment Metrics That Matter

"There has got to be more to a college education than vocational training," Sue mused. "Our graduates should be able to think, to cope with different points of view, to tell fact from fiction and ideology. Today, parents and students focus on what jobs graduates get and how much money they make. State funding rewards us for producing more STEM graduates, because they have better career prospects. We have to grow the programs that lead to good jobs, because the others are shrinking fast." Still, she wondered, "In twenty years, what will the consequences be? Is this just a passing trend?"

A s mentioned in the introduction, in 2009, Gray Associates made its first foray into employment metrics during our work with Universal Technical Institute, the world's largest school for auto mechanics (they have since expanded into other trades). When we began assessing academic programs for the institute, the number one priority was assuring strong career opportunities for their graduates. In part, we focused on opportunities for direct partnerships with large employers at a national level. This not only helped secure jobs for students but also opened the door for employers to fund program costs. However, most jobs were in local auto dealers and repair shops, so we also needed data on the jobs available in local markets, then and in the future.

Today, parents, students, and legislators are concerned with job prospects, so colleges of all types are paying closer attention to national and local employment statistics and the outcomes achieved by their own graduates. What data do they really need?

To start, it is useful to know how many people are employed in a given occupation or type of work (e.g., lawyers, marketing managers, or first-line supervisors of nonretail salespeople). As you would expect, occupations with a high number of employees usually have a high number of job postings.[7] The BLS conducts biannual employer surveys, similar to the US Census, to estimate the total number of people employed in an occupation. We believe this estimate is reasonably accurate, though it is somewhat dated (it takes a year to analyze and publish the survey results). It is reported at a granular level, down to the county, so it provides insight on national, state, and local employment.

Institutions would like reliable ten-year forecasts to inform long-term investments in programs. Most first-time students entering postsecondary education today will not graduate for two to six years (depending on degree level). For new programs, we need to add a year or two for the program to be developed and launched; therefore, its graduates will not hit the job market for four to eight years. To address this need, much of higher education relies on the BLS ten-year

---

7   There is an 88 percent correlation between BLS employment and the number of job postings by academic program (using Gray crosswalks from occupation to academic program). Gray analysis of Bureau of Labor Statistics 2020 employment survey, Gray job postings, September 1, 2020 through August 31, 2021.

forecast for estimates of future employment and job openings, which would make perfect sense if the forecast were accurate.

In our work, we began to unpack the forecasts for auto mechanics. Every two years, the BLS count of the number of auto technicians would decline at a predictable rate. Every two years, BLS would also forecast, and the forecast always predicted growth, which did not materialize for many years. (After years of decline, the occupation is now growing about 1 percent annually.)

We then back tested five years of BLS forecasts and found that 80 percent were off by 50 percent or more. To clarify, BLS misestimated the *growth rate* by 50 percent. Most annual growth rates are between 1 percent and 5 percent, so a 50 percent error is roughly a two-percentage point annual error in total employment. In our analyses, the trend in employment for the last three years is almost as accurate as the BLS forecast. In any case, it is worth remembering Yogi Berra's observation: "It's tough to make predictions, especially about the future." Few people predicted the pandemic and even fewer anticipated that it would lead to a boom in boat sales.

We continued to use BLS in our work but became more careful with the forecasts. In parallel, we began to look for more current sources and better insights on future hiring.

Job Posting Services

Job postings reflect the current reality (and a little of the past) and are a great complement to BLS. They are a more up-to-date indicator of how many people are needed to fill available jobs. They are also useful for career services staff and students looking for jobs.

However, the information can be skewed. Some job posting services pull data only from job boards, which like to leave up old job postings even if the job has been filled (job boards like to boast about the number of postings they have). Old posts could have several meanings. They could be jobs that are always in demand, jobs that are hard to fill, or jobs that have already been filled. Hospitals are almost always hiring a nurse of one kind or another, so they may have a posting open for months or years, but their job still needs to be filled. A three-month-old job posting for an accounts payable clerk may have been filled two months ago. There is no easy fix for this issue; filtering out old postings will screen out jobs that no longer exist but will also filter out jobs that are hard to fill.

To be more complete, some job posting services pull data from several job boards, employer sites, and other sources. This approach has its challenges: Old posts are included, and employers often post the same job in several places. There are services that use sophisticated natural language processing algorithms to remove the duplicates. While the algorithms are improving, deduping does introduce errors—some duplicate postings remain, and some unique postings are excluded by mistake.

Gray also draws data from approximately twenty-eight thousand websites of larger employers. Employers have no incentive to leave up postings for jobs that have been filled and seldom list the same job twice. On the other hand, it is quite a challenge to find the job pages on millions of small business websites. Further, many small businesses post openings on job boards but not on their websites. To address this issue, we gather small business openings from job posting services.

To gauge job market saturation, we calculate the number of postings per graduate in each program. The recent national average in our data sets is about 4.5 jobs per graduate. In a field with seven job postings per graduate, grads will have a better than average chance of finding a job. For programs with one or two postings per graduate, the job hunt will be more challenging. These ratios vary by program and location. It usually makes sense to focus on programs where your graduates will have a reasonable likelihood of finding a well-paid job.

The Crosswalk between Degree and Employment

The number of jobs available in fields related to a program is a starting point for employment analysis. We've talked about the two fundamental sources, BLS and job postings. Analysts then face a major issue: How do they determine which jobs align with which programs? Auto tech programs directly prepare students to become auto mechanics. Over 80 percent of nursing students go into nursing. So far, so good. But which occupations do business majors go into? CEO? General manager? Retail sales? The NCES publishes a crosswalk that aligns programs with jobs for which their students are directly prepared.

Let's look at the potential job market for a general degree like business. According to the NCES crosswalks, a business major is directly prepared to become a general manager, CFO, CEO, business analyst, or one of twenty-five other occupations. Let's assume there are one hundred thousand BLS job openings in these occupations. Do we assign them all to business majors? What about the accounting majors or finance majors who are also directly prepared for the occupations? Are the one hundred thousand jobs available to them, too?

If we assign all the jobs to each program, we'll end up claiming that three hundred thousand jobs are available, one hundred thousand each for business, accounting, and finance. Unfortunately, analysts who research a single program seldom recognize this problem:

They assume that all the jobs in related occupations are available to graduates of the program under study, substantially overestimating employment opportunities. To fix this error, jobs need to be split up and allocated among all the programs that prepare students for the occupation.

As I am sure you know, students are an unruly bunch. They do not read crosswalks, and many go into all sorts of fields for which they are not directly prepared. In particular, the majors from the much-maligned liberal arts often do not go into the fields for which they are directly prepared. NCES opines that history majors are only prepared to go into about ten fields (the number changes from time to time). These occupations include secondary school history teacher, secondary school teacher, historian, and "business, other." Not a lot of jobs there—or pay.

Does the NCES crosswalk reflect reality? Not really. NCES is honest about it: "The purpose of the crosswalk is to match postsecondary programs of study that provide graduates with specific skills and knowledge to occupations requiring those skills or knowledge to be successful. The matches are based on the content of the CIP Code and SOC Code descriptions combined with expertise from statisticians at both federal agencies. *The CIP SOC Crosswalk is not based on actual empirical data.*"[8]

According to the American Community Survey (the long form of the US Census), history majors go into over four hundred fields, about one hundred times as many as reported in the NCES crosswalk. Between the ages of thirty and sixty, history majors earn more than 76 percent of other majors and have unemployment rates that are about average (56th percentile).

---

8   National Center for Education Statistics, "CIP SOC Crosswalk," September 2021, https://nces. ed.gov/ipeds/cipcode/post3.aspx?y=56; emphasis is author's.

Crosswalks are often taken for granted, ignored, or grossly miscalculated. I suspect these errors underlie many of the popular misconceptions about degrees, jobs, and wages. Creating a good crosswalk takes considerable domain knowledge about programs and occupations. It is tedious work to align over one thousand academic programs, six degree levels, and seven hundred occupations—a matrix with 4.2 million cells. When you see data on employment for graduates of academic programs, ask where it comes from and how it was calculated. Be sure the underlying crosswalk reflects reality, not just the opinions of labor market economists.

It is easy to make massive errors aligning programs to jobs, errors that may underestimate or overestimate jobs by ten times or more. At Gray, we have spent years developing, refining, and deduping our crosswalks. We started with the NCES crosswalk and still use it for "direct prep" jobs. To complement this view, we also use data from the ACS survey to track the fields in which program graduates are actually employed and what they earn.

A Note on Wages

There is increasing pressure to make sure that students earn a good return on their investment in postsecondary education. To address this issue, program analysts should document the likely wages for graduates. Many of the sources for employment data also provide wage information. BLS provides good surveys of wages by occupation (you will also need a good crosswalk to align wages with programs). The American Community Survey is a more direct source of data on degrees and careers. It tracks income by academic program and age group, showing wages soon after graduation and in midcareer. Unfortunately, this survey tracks only results for bachelor's degree graduates. Glassdoor, job boards, and others also report wages. Be careful with wage data from job boards. Most job postings do not include wage information, so the sample may be small or biased.

Jobs for Philosophers?

We must also be careful about drawing ill-informed judgments about which programs have value in the workplace and which ones don't. To take it a step further, we should question how critical workplace value truly is.

Over the last five to ten years, there has been an increasing focus on the career outcomes of programs and a growing belief that many academic programs are not tightly aligned with healthy career outcomes, to the point of suggesting the elimination of some of the more generalized areas of education like history, philosophy, and literature. This path may diminish essential skills such as creativity and logic, which in turn may hinder innovation.

> We should question how critical workplace value truly is.

As an example, *Forbes* magazine recently proposed to name "chief philosophy officers" to corporate boards of directors. The first effects of this change in mentality have already arrived: The salary comparison site PayScale found that graduates with philosophy diplomas are better paid than their business administration peers. Silicon Valley start-ups are busy recruiting Stanford graduates who are "fuzzies" (humanities and liberal arts majors) who likely savor their long-anticipated victory over the techies. In a sign of the times, in 2021, celebrity investor Bill Miller donated an unprecedented $75 million to the philosophy department at Johns

Hopkins University. Jack Ma, the founder of Alibaba, said at the World Economic Forum in Davos, that education is going to be concentrated in areas that are not (yet) automated, such as critical thought and ethics.

I told the story of Google hiring philosophers at a conference, and afterward, a woman walked up to me, and she said, "I am that person. I was a philosophy major. I learned to code. Now those graduates with a degree in coding work for me."

Service Professions and the Arts

The analytical techniques presented thus far work well for most programs, but there are some where passion, societal needs, or mission are in conflict with the hard data. There are thousands of students interested in these social work programs. There are jobs for social workers—and widespread need for their support. However, wages are extremely low, making college debt and return on investment a real issue for these students. The arts routinely fail to meet thresholds for jobs and wages. Many are expensive to teach. Music courses often have among the highest instructional costs per student credit hour (SCH) at a university. Theater programs have similar characteristics—few jobs, low wages, and high instructional cost. In all these examples, the students and professors tend to have a passion for their programs that overshadows the hard realities of their fields.

The data we have discussed will provide context, but it will fall short for decisions about these programs. Each institution needs to come to grips with these programs in a way that is consistent with its own mission, culture, and resources.

A sound crosswalk is a cornerstone of program evaluation.

In summary, employment data, like all data, is messy. Employment predictions are needed but should be used with caution; simple trends may be better than most predictions. Crosswalks that connect employment data to programs are often overlooked, hard to develop, and prone to huge errors. A sound crosswalk is a cornerstone of program evaluation. Many constituencies focus entirely on employment outcomes; however, employment is just one aspect of program evaluation. To sustain enrollment and revenue, institutions still need students, who have their preferences and passions.

"It all seemed easy, before we got started," Sue thought, "then it became a mess. We could see the jobs and pay on job boards; we could even see the skills required. In most cases, the jobs and skills did not neatly align with a program, and some mapped to dozens of programs. And we still need a crystal ball to predict which jobs will be available when our students graduate."

For all the messiness, the data was still useful in highlighting programs with room to grow, some that could not justify the debt students would take on, and others with very few jobs.

It surprised her that humanities majors did have good career prospects, despite all the press; as she thought, there were more computer science jobs than there were grads—and entry-level coders were paid more than most faculty. Sue was still troubled by the programs that seemed so important to students and universities but that were likely to lead to unemployed or underpaid and heavily indebted graduates.

Many of the programs with strong employment outlooks were well known and highly competitive. Sue wondered, "Where are the gaps in competition that we can fill and give our grads a sound education that gets them started in good careers? Are there programs that have lots of competition that still have not reached their full potential?"

CHAPTER 5

Competitive Intensity and Market Saturation

"More student demand is better," Sue thought. "More job postings are better. But is more competition better or worse? Our biggest programs are offered by hundreds of universities—and at most of those universities, they are big programs, too. None of the big, successful online players earned their chops marketing small programs. They jumped into large markets and took share or attracted adult and other learners who were being overlooked by traditional schools. Maybe competition is an indication of program potential.

"But there must be a point of diminishing returns ... a point where it gets too expensive to recruit students or where graduates can't get jobs. How do I tell whether a program is big and healthy or overrun by competitors?"

As It Was

There have always been a few very prestigious national competitors in higher education who have no trouble filling their freshman classes or graduate programs. For these institutions, competition was and is not about winning enough students; it is about winning their share of the best students in the country and the world. Even the pandemic played to their advantage, increasing applications and reducing acceptance ratios.

For most colleges and universities, the traditional undergraduate competitive playing field was more local, often just a few dozen miles around their campus.[9] Overall, a few dozen miles around a campus usually captured over 80 percent of students, a home state included a few more, and a two- or three-state region accounted for the rest.

These small geographic markets limited competition to a few colleges or trade schools near a campus. Some students went away to high-prestige schools, and more attended the state flagship university. When the number of high school graduates was growing, this market structure made for a collegial competitive environment—there were plenty of students to go around.

As It Is

During the Great Recession, competition for employment emerged as a bigger issue, often fueling arguments about the value of a higher education and leading students to choose colleges and majors that had better odds of leading to a well-paid job. It made colleges realize that they competed in at least two types of market: student markets and job markets.

---

9   Ellen Wexler, "Geography Matters," *Inside Higher Ed*, February 3, 2016, https://www. insidehighered.com/news/2016/02/03/when-students-enroll-college-geography-matters-more-policy-makers-think.

In student markets, traditional undergraduate enrollment is now declining, intensifying competition for these students. Adult learners are a growth segment, but traditional colleges are often ill-equipped to serve them. In the adult market, national online giants have emerged who pull undergraduate and graduate students from local markets nationwide. In addition, online program managers (OPMs) have aligned with private and public nonprofit institutions. OPMs bring enormous resources and advanced skills to marketing and admissions for online programs. They attract thousands of students and make national players out of many regional public universities. These trends are increasing competition in local and national markets on-campus and online.

The job market was highly competitive for over a decade. Now, there are thousands of jobs going unfilled. It remains unclear how employers view online degrees, which may give an edge to on-campus colleges, which are usually well known to local employers. Longer term, job market competition will ebb and flow with each turn of the economic cycle.

In this context, barriers to entry or competition are like walls around a garden. For the garden's owners, they create a protected space; for others, the fruit of the garden is out of reach. As discussed, one of the barriers to competition, campus location, has eroded.

Fortunately, some programs offer barriers to entry of their own. For example, launching a prelicensure nursing program takes a lot of time and money. Accreditor and regulatory approvals take years. Equipment is expensive, especially patient simulation mannequins. Faculty and clinical opportunities are in short supply. It usually takes three years or more to get a program fully underway; once developed, the new program is subject to enrollment caps that limit its impact on other institutions.

If you are already offering programs with high barriers to entry, they protect you. They are a deterrent to developing some new programs, though it is worth remembering that the effort required to scale the wall is proportional to the protection it provides once you are inside. Barriers can also be created or destroyed by working with your accreditors and lobbying regulators or by building a brand.

Today, most programs of any meaningful size have many local and national competitors, so finding empty spaces in a market is unlikely. Many existing programs are in decline, and new program launches face tough competition. From a programmatic perspective, the questions are: Which programs have manageable barriers to entry and room to grow? Which ones are large but not yet saturated? How can I differentiate my program in a crowded market?

Identifying the Competition

The traditional source for program-specific data on competition is IPEDS, specifically its completion data. It will identify who your competitors are by program, how large their programs are, and how fast they are growing. With it, you can calculate your market share by program and see if it is growing or shrinking. IPEDS can also show if your competition has launched a new program, closed one, or gone out of business. IPEDS completion information is somewhat out of date, since it takes years to produce the first reported completion in a new program or to teach out an existing program. Despite these weaknesses, IPEDS is an unusually complete gauge of the number, size, and share of on-campus competitors; in many other industries, there is no comparable public source of data.

Using IPEDS local and national data, you can calculate some important program metrics. The easiest is simply the number of local, regional, and national competitors for a program. Don't let these numbers deter you; there are always competitors, and in larger programs, there are lots.

A more useful metric is the median program size, both for online programs and on-campus offerings. Median program size is a good indicator of the potential size of a new program and whether you are holding your own in an existing program. The median is more useful than the average, which is often skewed by a single large competitor (e.g., the local state university). If a faculty member tells you that with more funding they can attract seven hundred students to a program, you should check the median program size. If the median number of completions is eleven, you may want to inquire about the magic flute that is going to lead seven hundred students to your door.

When the median program size is still growing, it indicates that institutions are finding more students to fill their seats. In my view, this is a highly positive indicator. If it is shrinking, it often means the institutions in the market are having trouble filling seats—the student side of the market is becoming saturated. In both cases, you should look at the detailed data on completions by competitor to make sure the change in the median is not skewed by a new entrant, a school or program closure, or other anomalies.

There is a catch. As mentioned in chapter 3 on student demand, IPEDS mislocates most online completions, reporting them in the home market for the institution. If you are in Phoenix, the market will appear highly saturated by thousands of online completions from Grand Canyon University, the University of Phoenix, and ASU Online, even though the vast majority of these students are not in Phoenix. This reporting bias can be addressed using NC-SARA data for online student enrollment by institution and state of student residence. Here is an example that shows Gray Associate's relocation of University of Phoenix graduates from Phoenix to their home markets.

UNIVERSITY OF PHOENIX
IPEDS Completions Reported to HQ Market

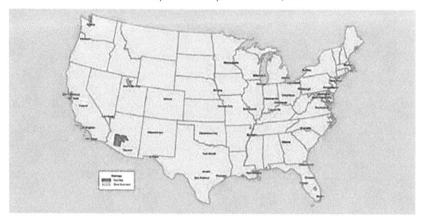

UNIVERSITY OF PHOENIX
PES+ Enhanced Completions by Local Market

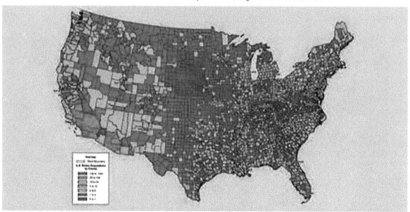

Sources: US Department of Education, National Center for Education Statistics, Integrated Postsecondary Education Data System (IPEDS), 2010 - 2020 Completions; National Council for State Authorization of Reciprocity Agreements

The analysis reveals who is really competing in local markets. For example, in the Washington, DC, market, according to IPEDS, the top two online competitors are George Washington University with 2,121 completions and Strayer University with 1,700. Both institutions have large national online programs, and the majority of their online students are not in DC.

Using NC-SARA, we found that the top three local competitors were not George Washington and Strayer; they were the University of Maryland Global Campus a half-hour drive north in Maryland, Johns Hopkins an hour away in Baltimore, and Walden University halfway across the country in Minnesota. Only the fourth-ranking competitor, George Washington University, was actually located in Washington, DC. As this example illustrates, the biggest national online institutions are significant competitors in local markets across the country, particularly in specific programs such as RN to BSN.

Nationally, there are several online institutions with over one hundred thousand students enrolled. They include Western Governors University, Southern New Hampshire University, the University of Phoenix, Grand Canyon University, and Liberty University. As a group, these institutions spend hundreds of millions of dollars a year on marketing. To understand their impact, my team monitors local Google search volume by institutional brand name. In one local market in Pennsylvania, Google search volumes for each "national" online brand were just 30 percent lower than the local colleges, a small gap that is likely to close as the online competitors continue to advertise throughout the country.

Many local colleges believe that demographic declines in high school graduates are eroding their enrollment. Demographics tell only part of the story. Western Governors had 83,000 students in 2015. They grew by almost 20,000 students in 2016 and another 20,000 in

2017. In 2018, they saw an increase of 25,000 and another 30,000 in 2019. In four short years, Western Governors' online enrollment grew from 83,000 to 175,000 students. They are adding more students per year than there are students in the entire public higher-education system in some states and more than are enrolled in most universities. They prove that it is possible to grow, despite demographics; many enrollment declines are more the result of competition, weak brands, poor marketing, and offering the wrong programs.

> Many enrollment declines are more the result of competition, weak brands, poor marketing, and offering the wrong programs.

The Competitors Not Found in IPEDS

IPEDS is not just missing data on local online competition; it also misses institutions that do not take federal financial aid. This is primarily an issue for less-than-degree programs and certificates. Dental Assisting programs are a good example. Dental Assisting is a relatively short program with strong job placement results and reasonable wages. There are franchised Dental Assisting programs that provide training in a dentist's office on Saturdays; the students pay by credit card. The programs do not receive Title IV funding, so they do not appear in IPEDS. The same is true for coding boot camps and other institutions that are paid with cash or private credit.

MOOCs are also not in IPEDS. MOOCs seemed to be a short-term fad after they lost media attention. But someone forgot to tell the MOOCs, which now offer more than sixteen thousand courses worldwide, and enrollment in some courses is enormous. Harvard's Computer Science 50 course is offered on edX and has enrolled over a million students. Few MOOC students will graduate or finish a program, so MOOC enrollment is not comparable to enrollment at a traditional college, but MOOCs remain a source of competition, especially for cutting-edge subjects and working adults.

Since MOOCs and their courses and programs are not accredited or regulated, MOOC courses are easy to start. If a student is interested in a cutting-edge course like quantum computing, they would be hard-pressed to find a related course at their local college or in most state universities. But they will find several courses on quantum computing on Coursera. On this platform, both students and instructors try out courses and programs, giving a window into future student demand and competition for emerging programs.

Determining Market Saturation

Higher education is becoming increasingly competitive, but competition doesn't always mean that a market is saturated. Depending on the institution, competition can be food or foe. Institutions with a strong brand name and a great marketing organization are going to seek out big, competitive markets because they know the students are there, and they can step into a market and take share from the existing institutions. For one of our clients, we found

> Higher education is becoming increasingly competitive, but competition doesn't always mean that a market is saturated.

that they took 50 percent market share when they entered a market. For them, competition was food.

Most colleges are not so fortunate and do not have the brand or marketing clout to take share in a saturated market.

There are several indicators you can use to determine whether a market is saturated, including cost per inquiry and Google cost per search. Institutions directly or indirectly bid for both inquiries and searches. The bidding drives up the cost in more competitive markets and programs. If these costs are well above average, the program market is getting highly competitive.

Google also offers the Google Competitive Index by keyword, which ranges from zero to one, with one being the most competitive. It's a good indicator of competitive intensity, especially if you compare an existing program you offer with a potential new program's index. If the new program's index is higher than you are accustomed to, program growth or market entry is likely to be a challenge. The index can also explain enrollment declines in existing programs.

Thus far, we have discussed the saturation of student demand. There are other dimensions of saturation that need to be addressed. Clinical sites for healthcare programs are often a constraint. Some institutions are skillful at winning clinical sites while others simply pay for them, but clinical sites may determine when a healthcare market is saturated. To the best of our knowledge, the only way to assess clinical saturation is to visit or call potential clinical sites to assess their interest.

Programmatic accreditors may also dictate when markets are full. There are a number of programs with waiting lists for students and employment shortages that are nonetheless capped by their accreditors. In these circumstances, it isn't the number of students who want the program or the number of jobs for graduates; it is the accreditor's perception of the program that determines who wins. As a result, accreditors' conferences are well attended by educators and senior executives who need to know what the accreditor requires and to form relationships with the leaders of the accrediting organizations. These insights on accreditors are a vital part of program evaluation in many fields.

Job opportunities for graduates may also be saturated. It would be unwise, both morally and from a regulatory perspective, for an institution to systematically recruit and graduate more students than there are jobs. At some point, regulators will discover low placement numbers and recent graduates' unpaid financial aid bills.

Within the employment data covered in chapter 4, there are a few metrics that indicate job market saturation, though none have hard cutoffs. Beware of using BLS's job opening estimate. It is derived from the BLS growth forecast and is highly inaccurate. One option is to create your own forecast; we have considered this approach and may yet give it a try. Unfortunately, any forecast of the future, even our own, is likely to be inaccurate, especially if the economy runs into a recession, pandemic, war, or other surprise.

BLS does provide the best available estimate of the number of people employed in an occupation. It also shows the actual growth in employment over time. The unit growth in employment (the annual change in the number of jobs) is part of the answer. It tells us how many new jobs are being created. However, it misses the number of jobs that must be filled to replace workers who quit, retire, or get promoted, which is usually larger than job growth.

For current data on the job market as a whole, the BLS Job Openings and Labor Turnover Study (BLS JOLTS) includes information on hiring, job openings (at the end of each month), and turnover (e.g., quits, layoffs, retirements, and discharges). Unfortunately, JOLTS data is captured by industry,[10] not by occupation; while it provides insight into the economy and general labor market trends, it would be very difficult to align with academic programs, so it is not very useful for program evaluation.

There is another publicly available option, the American Community Survey (ACS). While it is survey-based and lags the market quite a bit, ACS provides the unemployment rate, occupation, and wages by undergraduate program, gender, age, and ethnicity. This can give a college sound insight into the likely outcomes for students in current and potential new bachelor's degree programs.

For a more current indicator, twelve months of job postings provide a reasonable estimate of the number of people hired in a year. Given a few years of job posting data, you can also see if the number of people being hired is growing or shrinking. Then divide the annual number of job postings by the number of graduates per year to get the job postings per graduate ratio.

In 2010, before the anomalies introduced by the pandemic, the median job postings per graduate ratio in the US was between four and five. A number higher than four is relatively healthy. As the ratio approaches one, it is a warning that the labor market may be saturated.

There are exceptions, particularly in fields that prepare graduates for generalist positions where a bachelor's degree may be required, but the major is not important. For example, in psychology, there are substantially more bachelor's graduates than jobs; however, most psychology majors do not intend to become psychologists; they go into many other fields. As a result, the shortage of psychology-related jobs is not particularly important.

---

10   JOLTS data is collected and organized into the National American Industry Classification System (NAICS) and does not provide data by occupation.

In vocationally oriented fields and graduate programs, job postings per graduate are more relevant. Most prelicensure nursing program students want to become nurses (82 percent go on to nursing jobs). Most law school graduates expect a job practicing law for a company or law firm. In the case of nursing, state boards and accrediting bodies have limited the number of students, so there remain plenty of jobs for graduates; the job postings per graduate ratio was 4.2 (in 2021). In law, institutions have often produced more graduates than there are jobs. In 2021, there were just 0.6 job postings per graduate, which made job hunting a challenge for many graduates, despite the tens of thousands of dollars they invested in a degree.

Institutions bear some responsibility for these outcomes, good and bad. It is misleading and perhaps unethical to start or grow programs where job prospects are bleak, no matter how popular or profitable they may be. It is also somewhat addictive as colleges become dependent on programs that generate margins for the institution.

Fortunately, there remain programs in almost every market that have the potential to grow, increase institutional margins, and enable graduates to get good jobs. The goal is to add or grow programs in fields with high student demand, plenty of job openings, high wages, and healthy margins.

The dean of the history department, Henry Franco, attacked the proposed program in cybersecurity. "Sure it's growing, but everybody and their brother offers it. There are already over two hundred programs in the US, including three right in our backyard. The money could be better spent strengthening our core curriculum so that our graduates know how to think and write."

Where you stand depends on where you sit, Sue reflected. "Henry, there are quite a few cybersecurity programs, but the median program size is still growing, the Google Competitive Index is below average, and admissions has a steady flow of applicants who want to take the program and end up at another college. This program is competitive, but it is not saturated. I believe it could generate margins we need, which will also fund investments in our core curriculum. We'll need to estimate its margins before we can be sure."

CHAPTER 6

Program Economics

Dr. Harkins sputtered, "What the hell does margin have to do with what programs we offer? We are a university, not a business! We are here to expand the frontiers of knowledge and educate students, not to make money. As for evaluating faculty on how many student credit hours they teach or how much revenue and margin they generate, that is pure crap. You can't measure the quality of a professor by counting butts in seats."

Sue wondered how he could be so out of touch. The school was running a deficit. Its very existence was at stake, and here was Harkins ranting about the purity of academic purpose.

"Dr. Harkins," she replied, "we can ignore the economics of our programs. The economics will not ignore us. In a few years, we won't be here at all. We need to evaluate and improve the revenue, cost, and margins of our programs, precisely so that we can continue to teach them. If we managed our programs better, the margins generated by healthy programs could enable us to invest in the new program you want to teach. But now, underperforming programs consume the resources we need to invest in our growth and improve the quality of instruction."

"You haven't heard the end of this," he promised.

Indeed, he was quoted in the local papers a few days later, claiming that the university was planning to cut dozens of humanities programs without consulting the faculty. As far as Sue knew, no programs were yet on the chopping block. Her conversation with Dr. Harkins started as an invitation to help design and participate in a program evaluation process—that is, before she mentioned program economics and he stormed out.

Harkins had not been an initial supporter of using market data, either, but he did come around. "I'm confident he'll get comfortable with program economics once he understands them," Sue thought. For now, she wondered what she should say to the reporter who was waiting on her phone.

Some colleges and universities are born with the systems and culture to track and manage program economics. One of our Jesuit institutions developed its program economics reports well before we arrived. For-profits usually have this information as well, though many track profit by campus instead. Others develop the skills over time. In our informal surveys, about 40 percent of institutions have developed their own program profitability systems; however, these systems frequently confuse program and departmental economics and variable and fixed costs. Other institutions have program economics thrust upon them as their financials deteriorate. All too often, these institutions are plagued by program portfolios that drain resources, fail to attract students, and gradually decline in quality.

Understanding program economics is a vital part of fixing a program portfolio and running a healthy institution. Usually, the goal is not profit. The goal is to generate funds that the college can reinvest to advance its mission, strategy, and quality of instruction. A healthy program portfolio is a web of cross-subsidies from stronger programs to weaker mission-critical programs, growing programs that need funding, and new program launches that will increase enrollment and margins.

> Understanding program economics is a vital part of fixing a program portfolio and running a healthy institution.

What Are Program Economics?

Program economics should focus on the revenue, cost, and margin that a program decision is likely to change—what we call direct instructional margin. The analysis will include metrics that vary with short-term changes in student head count or faculty instructional time. The analysis will assign revenue, cost, and margin to sections, courses, and programs; it will exclude overhead.

Assigning cost or revenue differs from *allocating* them. Assigned costs vary with the work required to deliver education. If a program is added and students sign up for it, costs will usually rise to pay for sections and their instructors. In this case, the instructional cost is directly related to the program, more specifically to its courses and sections, and can be *assigned* to them.

Overheads are loosely or not at all related to student instruction. In the short term, the costs of the alumni office are largely independent of the number of students taught or the programs offered by the institution. Alumni office costs are not caused by programs, courses, or students, but they may be *allocated* to them, perhaps using the number of students enrolled or course credit hours.

Allocations spread overhead costs somewhat arbitrarily. Like spreading peanut butter on an English muffin, overhead allocations tend to smooth the real peaks and crannies of institutional economics. If we allocate overhead by student, large courses will inherit the lion's share of the cost, making them appear less profitable. If we allocate by program, small programs will get smothered in cost. Allocations also tend to generate resistance from whoever is being charged for them, since they did not cause the cost and cannot control it. In higher education, overhead is also a large percentage of cost, so it can quickly overwhelm program or departmental economics. To make matters worse, allocating overhead to programs can be misleading. If a program is shut down, the dean's travel will not change, nor will the chancellor's pay or alumni office staffing. The overhead will just be reallocated to other programs, which will make them look less profitable.

Given these issues, direct instructional margin does not include overhead allocations. Instead, it accounts for the factors that program decisions will change; it *assigns* all the revenue, cost, and margin that are directly related to teaching the program.

While program decisions do not change overheads, they do affect other departments. Business majors may be required to take English, which changes the economics of the English department.

Using direct instructional margin calculations, *program economics* moves the business majors' revenue and cost for English courses to the business program and subtracts them from the English department. In a departmental view, the economics of a business major taking an English course would stay in the English department. The departmental view is useful for staffing and budgeting; program economics should inform program decisions. Since program economics reach across departments, they are a challenge to calculate.

Conceptually, we assign a pro rata portion of a student's revenue (tuition and fees net of institutional scholarships) to the courses and sections in which the student is enrolled. We then assign a pro rata portion of a faculty member's wages and benefits to the courses they teach. We add in the other direct expenses that may be associated with a course, such as consumables used in labs. The pro rata revenues and costs of the course then follow each student into their program.

There are a couple of important additions to this conceptual approach. For state institutions, state funding often has two elements: per-student payments and institutional funding. We assign per-student funding to instructional revenue, courses, and programs. Institutional funding is excluded from program economics. It is used in higher-level analyses to offset overhead.

On the cost side of the ledger, it is important to distinguish between faculty time spent on teaching versus administration, research, and other activities. The nonteaching time is excluded from the cost of instruction and flows to departmental overhead. This calculation usually moves quite a lot of faculty cost (25 percent or more) from instruction to overhead. It also highlights the amount of money spent on nonteaching work and the amount of teaching capacity that is lost to nonteaching tasks. Often, the total nonteaching cost is a surprise to deans and the provost and can be a source of potential cost savings. We usually find that teaching, research, and release time do not account for 100 percent of faculty time; some leaks into the ether. This, too, may be a source of savings, insights into faculty work, or an opportunity to redirect the time into more productive activities.

Once you have calculated a professor's instructional cost, there is a question: Should it be assigned to the courses they teach or averaged across all the professors in the department? There is an argument that faculty assignments to courses are somewhat arbitrary. Within a department, a senior professor may teach a large introductory session one semester and an adjunct may teach it the next. If faculty are randomly switched from course to course, the average departmental cost for an instructor is a better metric than the actual cost of the instructor who happened to teach a course.

In practice, course assignments may not be random. More senior and expensive professors may be more likely to get assigned higher-level small courses and independent studies. This combination of small class size and high-cost professors can drive the cost per SCH through the roof (thousands of dollars per SCH is common). Using average cost per instructor would mask this issue. On the other hand, if you are estimating the cost of adding or deleting a program or course, the average may be more useful, since the effect on staffing may be uncertain. Of course, a good system could allow you to toggle between the average and the actual costs as needed.

Cross-listed courses add a layer of complexity. These courses may have a course number in each of two departments, but the students enrolling through one department appear to be taking a different course than the students who enroll under the other course number. The faculty member also appears to be teaching two courses, not one. In our early projects, cross-listed courses seemed to have very high costs per SCH, since each side of the listing would have half the students but would get assigned 100 percent of the teaching cost. We have learned to combine both sides of a cross-listing so that all the students are counted and so that faculty cost is not accidentally doubled.

In many cases, instructors are paid a flat fee to teach a course or an independent study. This is normal for adjuncts and quite common for professors who agree to take on overloads (extra courses) and independent studies. When this is the case, the actual fee paid should be used. The rationale is that the professor's average cost per credit hour is usually higher than the fee; if averages are used, it may lead to hiring adjuncts when a professor might be less expensive and happy to receive the extra pay. Actuals also enable deans to perceive and align higher-cost resources with courses and programs that can afford them and to ensure that these higher-cost resources sustain appropriate teaching loads. Overall, I prefer actuals because they show how things really are, without smoothing or averaging.

If you are interested in the math behind program economics, the following is a description of the calculations involved. The work is best done in an SQL database or business intelligence application (we use Qlik) because the files quickly become too large for Excel. To do this work, you will also need help and data from institutional research, finance, the bursar's office, human resources (specifically your payroll administrator), and others.

If you are not interested in the detailed mechanics of program economics, you can safely skip ahead to the Program Economic Analysis: Lessons Learned section later in this chapter.

Calculating Program Revenue

Students often choose a program that interests them, then they search for a college that has the program. If the program is not offered, they search for a different college. This search pattern is particularly true for more career-oriented programs (e.g., nursing), graduate programs, and adult learners. These student choices drive tuition revenue; therefore, revenue should be assigned to the programs and courses a student selects.

It takes big files to line up students, revenue, sections, courses, and programs. First is a list of all students, including their student IDs. Note that it is worthwhile to hash (disguise) their IDs in the program economics system so that their personally identifiable information is not accessible on the platform. Then pull tuition, fees, and institutional scholarships for each student ID by semester. This information should be available from institutional research, finance, or the bursar's office. Since the university does not fund them, Pell Grants and other external scholarships need not be included.

A few more files are required: the number of credit hours per course and each student's enrollment by section, course, and program. With this data, you can calculate gross revenue (tuition and fees) and revenue net of discounts and scholarships for each student and assign them to classes and sections.

Some may argue that scholarships and discounts should just be averaged across students and their courses because it is challenging to align student scholarships with a student's courses and programs. Others may contend that these decisions are usually not made by the department, so it is unfair for departments to bear a disproportionate amount of the cost. Averaging discounts and scholarships is a serious mistake, as scholarships vary by student, from full rides to none at all; further, scholarship students tend to cluster in specific programs. As a result, total discounts vary widely by program; at one college, they ranged from $350 to zero, as shown next. Averaging them will seriously distort the real economics of your programs.

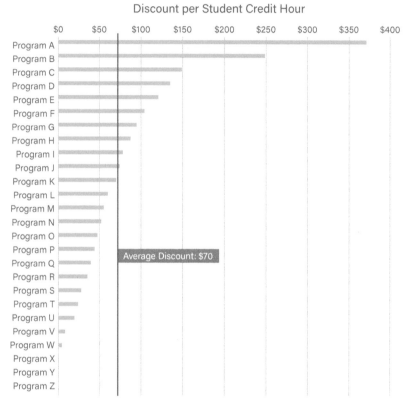

PROGRAM ECONOMICS
Discount per Student Credit Hour

Source: Gray Associates Benchmarking Database

Revenue and discounts are assigned to courses by student, using the number of credit hours per course. Let's consider an example:

A. Student: John

B. Major: Business

C. John's total tuition: $7,000

D. Minus John's institutional scholarship: $1,000

E. John's net tuition paid: $6,000

F. John's total course credit hours (CCH): 6

G. John's revenue per CCH: $1,000 (E/F)

H. Course: English

I. English CCH: 3

J. English course net revenue from John: $3,000 (G*I)

In program economics, John's revenue and cost for the English course would roll up to his business program. In a departmental view, it would flow to the English department. For program decisions, such as whether to keep or cut a program, you should use program economics, since it will correctly calculate all the effects of the program change, not just those in the home department. For staffing the English department, a departmental view would be more appropriate. Departments manage teaching capacity and efficiency; programs generate revenue and use capacity.

Later, you will want to calculate the difference in revenue and margin by department, campus, and online, so you should collect the course department and campus ID, including online. You may also want to see how metrics vary by student type, so it is worth pulling gender, ethnicity, age, Pell status, level (e.g., freshman), and enrollment status (e.g., withdrawn) for each student.

Calculating Direct Instructional Cost

More data is needed to calculate direct instructional cost by section, course, and program. The data includes faculty IDs (which should be hashed) and the courses taught by each faculty member. Payroll should be able to provide salaries and benefits by faculty ID. You should also collect nonwage costs that vary with the number of students taught, such as lab supplies for biology. In some cases, these charges are substantial—airline pilot training programs may use over $100,000 a year in gasoline. We consider capital investments, such as buildings and labs, as overhead and do not include them in direct instructional costs.

Once you have all the instructional costs, you can use course credit hours to assign the costs to programs. As with revenue, you simply divide the cost of each faculty member by the total number of CCHs they teach to get their cost per CCH taught. Each course a faculty member teaches is then assigned the faculty member's cost per CCH. Let's continue with our English course example, which is taught by Dr. William James:

A. Instructor: Dr. William James

B. Dr. James's annual salary: $100,000

C. Dr. James's health and retirement benefits: $20,000

D. Employer-paid payroll taxes: $13,333

E. Dr. James's total compensation: $133,333 (A+B+C)

F. Share of Dr. James's time spent teaching: 75 percent

G. Dr. James's teaching costs: $100,000 (E*F)

H. Dr. James's total CCHs: 10

I. Dr. James's cost per CCH: $10,000 (G/H)

J. Course: English

K. Faculty: Dr. W. James

L. CCH: 3

M. Course faculty cost: $30,000 (I*L)

N. Other direct cost: $1,000 (for online library access)

O. Total instructional cost: $31,000 (M+N)

At present, few colleges undertake activity-based cost analysis to assign direct costs for shared instructional expenses, such as student services; however, these costs are rising. For now, the ongoing costs of collecting cost by course and program may outweigh the benefits. As program economic analysis matures, techniques will be developed to accurately and efficiently determine the time and cost of shared resources by program. For example, using artificial intelligence, a system could analyze emails, texts, and calls to track student support time spent by course and program. In the meantime, it is reasonable to *allocate* student support costs to courses using SCHs, since these costs will vary by student; we just do not yet know how to accurately *assign* them.

Direct Instructional Margin

Perhaps the easiest calculation in the analysis, direct instructional margin, is simply instructional revenue minus instructional cost. It measures the money a program contributes to or draws from departmental and institutional funds. It is essential to track margin, since many high-cost programs also generate high margins; cutting these high-cost programs would inadvertently reduce revenue and margin, making finances worse. You may also want to calculate return on program expenses (RoPE): program margin divided by program costs. RoPE gives you a sense of the returns you should expect on each dollar of instructional cost.

Program Economic Analysis: Lessons Learned

We have completed a few dozen program economics projects, and our benchmarking data set now includes over 1,800 programs of all sizes. We have learned a great deal about what makes educational economics tick and have been surprised by many of the findings. For example, when we started this work, we expected to find that most small programs would have negative margins.

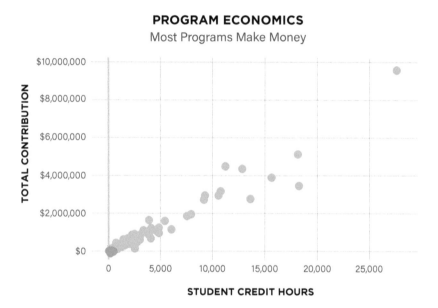

PROGRAM ECONOMICS
Most Programs Make Money

In fact, almost all programs make money, even small ones; to be more precise, they generate margins that help to pay for departmental and institutional overhead. This is not to say that they generate enough margin to cover all overhead, but they do help. More specifically, only 12 percent of programs in our data set have negative margins. Even among small programs with fewer than one thousand SCHs per year, only 19 percent have negative margins—that is, 81 percent of very small programs have positive margins that help to pay for overhead. If you accidentally cut small contribution-positive programs, you may find that the savings from cutting faculty are more than offset by declines in enrollment and tuition. There remain programs that have missed their sell-by date and should be sunset, but there is usually no pot of gold at the end of the teach-out. There are caveats.

Shifting students to other majors: If you can switch students in a sunset program to another program, you can retain their revenue while realizing the cost savings. If you cannot switch them, you may be stuck with the cost of teaching out programs, which can take years. If you have to teach out a program, joining a course-sharing network, such as Acadeum, that can teach the remaining students and courses, will usually lower cost per student, since the instructor cost is shared among several colleges.

Cannibalization: Some programs appear to make money, but a deeper analysis may reveal that they are cannibalizing students and margins from other programs. This is a particularly complex issue for new programs. Often new programs attract students who may have enrolled in an existing program—increasing instructional cost without increasing revenue. In a recent discussion with a small private college, their data science program appeared to be quite successful while their business program was declining by exactly the same number of students. This shift suggested that the new data science program did not draw in new students; it just took them from business. Nonetheless, offering data science *may* have been the right move, serving to retain the data science students who might have otherwise chosen a different college.

Attractors: There are programs that can attract more students than they can teach. Premed programs often draw students who cannot get through organic chemistry. Engineering attracts some students who find that they cannot keep up and switch to another major. It is important to have programs that provide off-ramps for these highly attractive but selective programs. It may also be worthwhile to track the economics of these students in the major that brought them into the institution, in addition to the major in which they ended up.

The outcome of program economic analysis is not always intuitive to me. Using our benchmarking data, we calculated the average margin per SCH across over 850 programs at sixteen institutions (see the following figure). You may expect that programs with lower-cost faculty and lots of general education courses, like history and English, would have above-average margins. Both have below-average margins—history is almost 10 percent lower than average, and English trails the average by over 20 percent. Computer science, which has to compete for professors with highly paid private sector jobs, still manages to produce margins that are more than 10 percent above average. Nursing, which has notoriously high costs and class sizes that are often constrained by accreditors, has margins that are 40 percent above average.

Your program margins are likely to be different from many of our benchmarks. Please don't guess or use rules of thumb, which are likely to be wrong and are certainly unnecessary. Program economic analysis allows you to know which programs are contributing to your institution's financial health and which ones need help to survive.

> Program economic analysis allows you to know which programs are contributing to your institution's financial health and which ones need help to survive.

WHICH PROGRAMS GENERATE ABOVE-AVERAGE MARGINS?
Difference from Average Program Margin per SCH
(Bachelor's programs offered by four or more institutions)

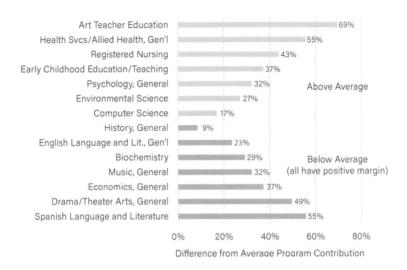

Difference from Average Program Contribution

Variation is another hallmark of program economics (and curricular efficiency). In a well-run production facility, the cost to produce a part is highly predictable, but the cost may not have been so predictable when the part was first introduced. During the early stages of production, considerable time is spent refining the process, reducing cost, and improving reliability so that the part is consistently the same size, shape, and cost. This level of engineering does not seem present in higher education. As a result, the revenue, cost, and margin for programs and courses are startlingly different. Recently, a client and I reviewed their cost per SCH by course. Their norm was around $300 per SCH. The highest was $2,500 and the lowest was under $100 per SCH—the most expensive course cost twenty-five times more per SCH than the least expensive. When we filtered to include only courses at the same level (e.g., 400-level courses), the variation remained. As it turned out, at the high end, a full professor was teaching a class with two students, despite an institutional policy that all courses have at least six students.

In manufacturing, a process with a high degree of variation is referred to as out of control: It has not yet been engineered well enough to be predictable. Higher education is intrinsically a complex process; bringing it under "control" is likely to prove difficult, and a high degree of cost control may not even be desirable. In theory, cost controls may stifle the creativity and innovation that is needed for students and institutions to flourish. Perhaps the level of control should vary by type of institution, program, student, and funding—but not by accident. The curriculum for some programs is well defined, often by programmatic accreditors, and they attract enough students to accurately predict enrollment. The desired outcomes may be defined by formal tests and certifications, such as state bar exams and the NCLEX exam for nursing. In these cases, it would make sense to have predictable processes that produce the target outcomes at lower cost. The same level of predictability may be more difficult to achieve in less defined fields, like history or undergraduate psychology. While the ideal level of process control and predictability may vary, from what we have seen, there is plenty of room for improvement in almost every institution, department, and program.

If the results of margin analysis vary widely and are often counterintuitive, what drives them? Why do they differ from our expectations? Chapter 7 describes the drivers of curricular efficiency, which are an important contributor to process predictability and program margins. For those who are drawn to Zen-like metaphors, a cactus thrives in the desert while a maple tree dies in a drought because it has many more branches and leaves. For a less Zen explanation, the more courses you offer, the more likely that cost per SCH will be high and unpredictable.

Overhead—At Last!

Once you have a firm grasp on program economics and direct instructional margins, it is time to turn to overhead. Academic programs must produce enough margin not only to pay for instruction but also to support the institutional activities that enable education to occur. It is not helpful for faculty to think that any positive margin is enough. For many institutions, average margins need to be three times instructional cost—that is, three dollars of revenue for every dollar spent on instruction.

This is not unusual. Often the direct cost of delivering a product or service is a small fraction of the total cost of operating an enterprise. In telecommunications, the physical cost of running the network may be less than 10 percent of total cost. In publishing, the author receives a small percentage of the revenue on their book. In software, the cost of delivering an application to a user is approximately zero. In higher-education institutions, there are large and growing overheads being driven by everything from facilities operations and maintenance to regulatory compliance, financial aid administration, and student mental health.

For program economics, simpler overhead analysis is usually better. Spending academics' time analyzing and disputing overhead allocations is not particularly useful, though constant pressure to control overhead is constructive. In this spirit, the simplest version of overhead analysis subtracts the direct instructional cost collected in program economics from the general costs and revenue of the university. Overhead is the result.

There are quite a few ifs, ands, and buts to this calculation. In particular, the costs and revenue of noneducational ancillary activities should usually be excluded. These may include a university hospital system, café, or solar power facility. Alternatively, one could include net gains or losses from ancillary activities. The critical number is educational overhead as a multiple of cost (total educational overhead divided by total instructional cost). Let's assume that there is $30 million in overhead cost and $10 million in instructional cost. The resulting overhead multiple would be 3.0 ($30M/$10M). In this case, the margin target for academic programs must be at least 3.0 times educational expense to sustain the institution. This approach enables institutions to set simple, understandable targets for academic margins.

One flaw in this calculation can be fixed with departmental multiples that take into account variation in departmental overheads. In its simplest form, departmental overhead boils down to the pay for the deans and their assistants. In practice, it is a little more complicated. Many deans spend time teaching, which would be assigned to direct instructional cost. Conversely, a substantial chunk of faculty cost was excluded from direct instructional cost; this noninstructional cost becomes a part of departmental overhead. Typically, faculty nonteaching costs will dwarf the pay of the dean and their assistants, so it will now get some long-overdue but generally unwelcome attention.

How much decanal and faculty nonteaching expense is too much? To answer this question, we would compare departmental cost per SCH across the university. Unlike teaching, where there are structural differences in cost per SCH (e.g., because of accreditor rules for maximum class size), there are fewer structural reasons for departmental cost per SCH to vary. Most variation is the result of managerial decisions. Comparing departmental costs per SCH should reveal genuine differences in overhead efficiency—and inefficient overhead is a poor use of institutional resources. As external benchmarks become available, they should also be used to evaluate the efficiency of departmental spending.

In combination with data on your markets, program economics will allow you to find big, high-margin programs in growing markets that you may be able to expand as well as small programs that may be losing money but that are in attractive, growing markets. These may warrant investment. On the other hand, money-losing programs in weak markets are likely to be bad bets—unless they are central to the institutional mission.

Calculating economics by program turned out to be more work than Sue expected. Doing a first draft had taken the university over a year. Cleaning it up with the deans took another six months and nearly undermined the whole effort as the deans found substantial errors and claimed the numbers were worthless. Basic cross-checks had been skipped, so the faculty cost in the economic model appeared to exceed actual faculty expense. The cost of cross-listed courses was calculated incorrectly, so they appeared exorbitantly expensive. Courses taught on overload pay were charged at full rates.

Harkins gloated, "The bean counters really got this wrong. What a waste of time and money. Money we could have spent giving hardworking faculty a raise last year."

The bean counters persisted, and as the calculations were corrected, Sue and the deans became more comfortable with the accuracy of the numbers and began to explore them. Sue had found several high-margin programs that still had room to grow. Deans were surprised to find just how much faculty time and cost was tied up in nonteaching work and how much was unaccounted for, lost in dribs and drabs that added up to millions of dollars.

The most disappointed person was the chancellor. As she said to Sue, "This doesn't make sense. Almost all our programs are contribution-positive, so cutting them won't improve our budget shortfall. Nonetheless, our enrollment and revenue have declined, and the cost of instruction has not. How do we get our costs in line? What do I tell the board?"

Sue replied, "First, please let them know that cutting programs won't help us much. That said, we can reduce costs. As I dug through the numbers, I found over a million dollars in potential cost savings, but it was not at the program level."

CHAPTER 7

Curricular Efficiency

"Where's the money?" Sue had asked herself as she went through the program economic analysis. Then she noticed a pattern: Almost all programs made money, but many courses did not. She began digging in at the course level and found dozens and dozens of courses with three to five students in them and cost per student credit hour well over $500, more than double the institutional average.

"Almost no one comes here to take a particular course," Sue thought. "If we prune a few of these tiny classes, enrollment and tuition will stay the same, but teaching loads and costs will fall. And what is all this release time and these hours that are not accounted for at all? Why is the departmental cost per student credit hour twice as high in nursing as it is in the humanities?"

n its basic form, curricular efficiency measures, manages, and improves the units of education that can be delivered for a given amount of instructional cost and quality. The metric we recommend, as a start, is cost per student credit hour. The latter part of the chapter introduces metrics that balance cost and quality of instruction.

The math for calculating instructional cost per SCH is simple: instructional cost divided by SCH taught. This metric enables reasonably accurate comparisons across institutions, departments, programs, course levels, and courses. Let's start at the bottom of this stack, with instructional cost per SCH.

Policy Decisions

As described in chapter 6, instructional cost is faculty wages and benefits, net of wages and benefits for nonteaching time, plus any consumables (e.g., lab supplies) used in the course. In this context, cost refers to what the institution pays to deliver a course, not what a student pays to take the course. Policy decisions heavily influence total instructional cost, the numerator of cost per SCH. These decisions also influence the denominator, setting guidelines for course credit hours and students per course.

Wage levels are set in periodic policy decisions and are difficult to change in the short term. Wages for unionized faculty may be set for years under a collective bargaining agreement. While they are subject to great debate, changes in wages and benefits are often small from year to year; in theory, rising labor costs could be offset by improving efficiency.

Required course credit hours: Policies also determine the number of course credit hours a faculty member should teach. The expectation varies widely, from zero for a prestigious researcher who wins a substantial grant, to eight courses and twenty-four course credit hours per year for a typical community college professor.

Rounding: Institutions may have policies on how to manage faculty loads when they do not divide evenly by standard course credit hours. A faculty member at one institution may be able to round up eleven course credit hours and declare that they have met their twelve-credit-hour target in a given semester. At another, they may be required to round down and teach an entire additional three-credit course (for a total of fourteen course credit hours) to satisfy a twelve-credit-hour requirement.

Minimum students per class: Many institutions have policies on the minimum number of students that must be in a class or section. Institutions may have the data and willpower to enforce these rules, or they may not have policies or timely reports to identify small courses before the add/drop date, or they may simply be unwilling to take on faculty and close small classes. Loose management of class size comes at a substantial cost.

As illustrated here, hundreds of courses may run with under five students, driving up cost per SCH. I am frequently surprised by the number of courses with just one student. However, most are independent studies, and faculty often receive little or no pay for overseeing this work. Excluding courses with one student, in the following example, over one hundred tiny courses remain; the cost to deliver these courses often exceeds $1,000 per SCH.

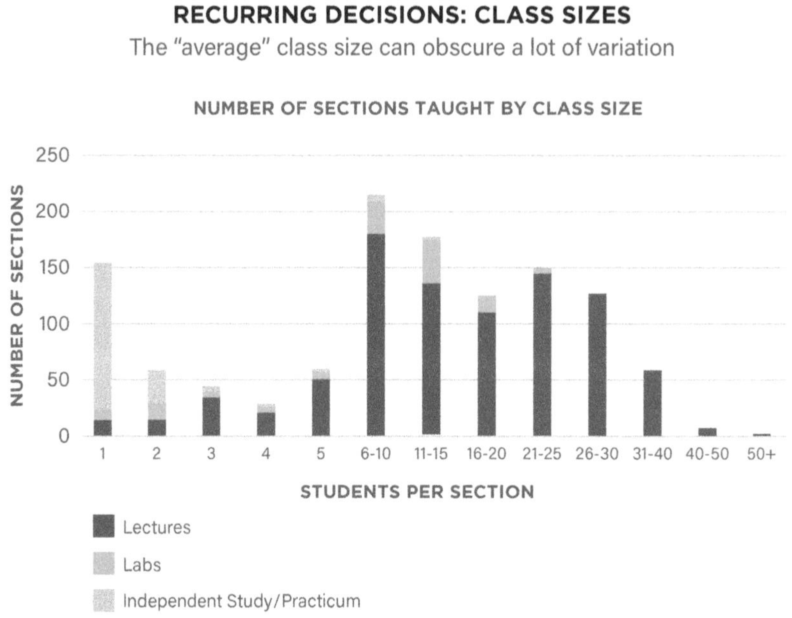
RECURRING DECISIONS: CLASS SIZES
The "average" class size can obscure a lot of variation
NUMBER OF SECTIONS TAUGHT BY CLASS SIZE
NUMBER OF SECTIONS
250
200
150
100
50
0
1
2
3
4
5
6-10
11-15
16-20
21-25
26-30
31-40
40-50
50+
STUDENTS PER SECTION
Lectures
Labs
Independent Study/Practicum

Number of courses and sections offered: Curricular sprawl is a pervasive problem. As mentioned, courses with low enrollment persist. Even courses that pass the minimum enrollment requirement may just cannibalize students from other courses. Faculty are paid to teach summer courses with low enrollment, even though the students could take the same course in the fall at no incremental cost. Cutting back the overgrowth could lower cost, free up full-time faculty, displace adjuncts, and enable faculty to focus on teaching fewer courses better. Below the course level, section sizes also vary widely, even within the same course.

Here are techniques you can use to make the course portfolio more efficient.

- *Cycle courses.* Related courses can be put on a cycle rather than teaching each one every term. For example, one university had three 300-level courses in a program for certain students.

They changed some requirements so that the courses could be taken in any sequence rather than as prerequisites for each other and then rescheduled them so that only one of the courses would be taught each term. Students could take all three in the order in which they were available. This change eliminated two sections of teaching each term in a relatively small department.

→ *Consolidate content.* Courses with similar content can be combined within a department or across departments. The iconic example is introductory statistics. At many institutions, there are introductory statistics courses covering similar content in several departments: math, business, social sciences, and others. A few Gray Associates clients have already consolidated these courses, and several others are considering it.

→ *Limit net new course sections.* Adding courses usually increases faculty workload and cost but not revenue. Very few students select a university for a single course; nonetheless, the new courses must be taught, increasing workload. On the other hand, the difference in cost between adding a course and adding a section may be modest, so curricular efficiency depends more on the number of course sections and less on the number of courses. If a new course draws one or more full sections from other courses, it may not add cost at all. Please note that rapidly changing disciplines (e.g., software development) may need a steady flow of new courses to keep up with evolving languages and applications. In these fields, phasing out courses on dying technologies is critical to maintain efficiency.

→ *Prune courses and sections.* At every institution, there exist courses and sections that are sparsely attended, poorly taught, or unimportant to their discipline. Pruning these courses reduces cost and better focuses faculty attention.

→ *Reduce independent studies.* Faculty usually receive much lower pay per credit hour for teaching independent studies, but they do take faculty time, which is directly or indirectly paid for through releases, negotiated standard course loads, or diversion of faculty time from other valuable activities like advising, service, or research. Proliferating independent studies may be a symptom of other issues, such as too few course sections to allow students to graduate, poor advising on course schedules, or independent studies that are not needed or appropriate for the student.

→ *Revise general education courses.* Gen ed courses are intended to provide students with a well-rounded baseline education; unfortunately, they may also be used to ensure enrollment in small courses and protect their faculty.

Let's consider which of these policy decisions is likely to have the greatest influence on curricular efficiency and cost. Wage increases usually range from 0 to 5 percent annually (though they may increase if inflation rises). Rounding policies can clean up 5 to 10 percent of faculty capacity and cost. Then we have faculty credit hour production and class size requirements. Increasing average course credit hours per professor from an average of six courses per year to seven, while increasing students per class from fifteen to seventeen, would lower cost per SCH by 20 percent. All these improvements could be amplified by pruning unneeded courses.

Is this level of improvement feasible? Here is a realistic illustration of class credit hours per instructor. Over two hundred faculty members are running substantially below the standard load of eighteen course credit hours. Other faculty members demonstrate that faculty could deliver more than eighteen course credit hours: Approximately two hundred professors deliver twenty-one to twenty-four credit hours. To me, there appears to be ample room to improve. In this case, as in many others, sound policy decisions could significantly reduce cost per SCH while focusing faculty attention on more vital courses and their students.

EFFECTIVE COURSE LOADS
Standard loads are seldom the standard

FULL-TIME FACULTY COURSE LOADS
Course Credit Hours Taught per Year
Fall & Spring Semesters

Day-to-Day Decisions

Tactical, day-to-day decisions are also important, including faculty mix, course scheduling, and section size.

Faculty mix: Wage levels vary by type of instructor (adjunct, lecturer, tenure track, or tenured). Changing the mix of instructors to use lower-cost faculty is relatively quick; the provost, deans, or chairs may be able to make changes every semester. The cost difference is substantial: A typical adjunct may be paid $3,000 per course while our Dr. Low clocks in at $10,000 per course ($80,000 in wages and benefits divided by eight courses per year). Many institutions have aggressively used adjuncts and lecturers to lower costs. Low-price online and for-profit institutions only use adjuncts as instructors. Beware: a "low-cost" instructor who causes just one student to drop out costs the school tens of thousands of dollars in lost revenue.

Release time and ratchets: The provost, deans, and others give faculty release time (reduced teaching loads) for a variety of reasons. For example, a professor may be given release time for a special project or for becoming a department chair. As time passes, the project may end or the faculty member's role may change. In theory, the release time should end, and the faculty member should resume a full teaching load. In practice, release time may not be well tracked or managed. It tends to be on a ratchet—it goes up, but it seldom comes back down; instead, it becomes a permanent tax on instructional capacity. In the following example, the institution pays $1.3 million per year for release time, 15 percent of total faculty compensation.

ROOM FOR IMPROVEMENT?

Release time and undocumented time cost millions

ILLUSTRATIVE FULL-TIME FACULTY COSTS
Small Liberal Arts College

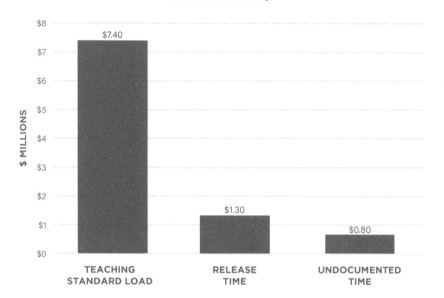

Lost time: There are faculty credit hours that fall between the cracks. As mentioned previously, a faculty member may fall a credit or two short of their required load. In other cases, a few faculty members may be several courses below the required load. For Dr. Low and Dr. High, the cost per credit hour is $3,333, so two missed credit hours is a $6,666 drop in faculty capacity. Unused release time has the same cost. Closer monitoring of workload and release time could increase faculty time available for teaching.

Marginal cost per course: It is sometimes more expensive for an adjunct to teach a course than a tenured professor. If Dr. Low were only teaching nine of twelve required course credit hours, the marginal cost for Dr. Low to teach three more credit hours is zero. An adjunct may cost an incremental $3,000. To lower institutional costs, many colleges should enable faculty to get back to teaching. Colleges may also use overload time and pay for professors, which is often comparable to adjunct pay.

Marginal cost for administration: In the nineties, when I did restructuring work, we usually found that consolidating administrative tasks and assigning them to a few people improved quality, reduced cost, and sped up processes. In contrast, talented faculty are often drawn into part-time administrative roles. It is worth considering whether these roles could be better done and at lower cost by paid administrators or contractors (the adjuncts of administration). Faculty could then focus on what faculty do best: research and teaching.

Accounting for Consequences

Enrollment in higher education is flat or declining. Declining enrollment combined with higher levels of curricular efficiency will reduce the number of required teaching faculty. Each institution must find ways to handle these cuts with grace and recognize the decades that many faculty have dedicated to the institution and their students. One of our clients offered normal retirement benefits and allowed retiring professors to keep an office and teach one course per semester (at adjunct rates).

All instructors are not created equal. Some inspire, clearly deliver complex material, provide constructive feedback, and encourage students. Others mail it in. Adjuncts face substantial challenges. Their pay is so low that they have to take on as many courses as they can stand, cutting into the time available to support students. Whether adjunct or tenured, we should not measure faculty productivity just by SCH delivered and cost per SCH.

The number of students in a course and SCH are usually measured on the add/drop date for a course. This approach measures how many students start in a course, not how many finish it. In effect, this is like measuring productivity at an auto manufacturing plant on how many parts come in, not how many cars go out. Shouldn't we measure successful course completions as well?

The cost of student failure eclipses the savings that can be achieved with curricular efficiency. In our conversations, academic leaders suggest that many students who drop out of a course also drop out of college. For a college that charges just $10,000 per year, every freshman who drops out reduces revenue by $10,000 per year, or $40,000 over the course of a four-year degree. For many colleges, tuition is several times higher, as is the lost revenue. At the margin, cost remains the same, so the lost revenue directly reduces institutional income.

Productivity metrics should encourage retention, not just enrolling students who start but do not finish. SCH and cost per SCH are still useful indicators. A simple addition would be student credit hours *completed* (SCHC) and cost per SCHC, which would measure efficiency and effectiveness. The percentage of students who successfully complete a course (SCHC percent) would also be useful, as it would measure the ability of the instructor to deliver the material in a way that enables students to succeed. Low SCHC or SCHC percent should be analyzed to determine whether the instructor is effectively delivering the material. However, it could also motivate faculty to lower grading standards and push students through who have not mastered the material, suggesting that an unusually high SCHC percent should be explored to ensure that grading is not too lenient.

> The cost of student failure eclipses the savings that can be achieved with curricular efficiency.

Enrollment

It is extremely difficult to improve productivity when fewer students are starting in college. Faculty may be able to influence the size of entering classes, perhaps by teaching a class at local high schools so that students believe they can take on college and that it will be interesting. Arizona State University reaches all the way down to grade school to persuade underserved students that they are welcome at ASU and can succeed there.

Faculty have a more direct influence on retention. Not every student can be retained; life often gets in the way, especially for underserved students. But more students could be retained, with adjustments to teaching styles, student support, modalities, content, and courses. A small improvement could have a significant impact on enrollment, tuition revenue, cost per SCH, and, especially, cost per SCHC and SCHC percent. Improving retention could offset declines in new students and sustain the health of many institutions and their faculty.

Most important, improving retention could reduce the enormous social cost of college dropouts. Dropouts accumulate student debt. Their résumés are impaired. They have little to show for years of their life and work. Their self-esteem may be damaged. All these costs disproportionately affect groups that tend to have lower completion rates, including underserved students, Black and Hispanic communities, and men.

In the long term, improving cost per SCHC would enable institutions to stop increasing prices and perhaps even lower them, which could make college more affordable. Improving student retention would increase institutional enrollment, revenue, and margins and sustain faculty head count. Improving retention would also lower the cost per SCHC and graduation rates. These improvements would further the mission of higher-education institutions and the health of our society.

If enrollment is flat or declining, improving faculty productivity will lead to reductions in faculty. And again, each institution must find ways to handle these cuts with grace and recognize the faculty members' many years of service.

"That was not fun," Sue thought as she reviewed the results of the curricular efficiency initiative, "but it was essential."

After a few months of detailed reviews, course by course and section by section, Sue and her deans had cut dozens of courses and sections while focusing each department on the content critical to its discipline. They had found millions of dollars of excess cost, some of which would be invested in student support to improve retention. Unfortunately, it also meant that some faculty would be let go. She was designing a plan that would enable most of them to retire with dignity and recognition for their many years of service. She felt for the more junior faculty and adjuncts, who would not have such generous packages.

She could cope with the pain she would create. "I should do what's right for the students and our community. I have to stop the inexorable increases in our instructional costs and tuition and focus our resources on equitable student success, enabling every group of students to get a sound education, graduate, and get a job—all at a reasonable cost. If I do that, it will also balance the budget and ensure the university's survival."

CHAPTER 8

Program Planning, Evaluation, and Management

The university completed its program evaluation and curricular efficiency work, and the results were starting to come in. Sue's team saved over $2 million by tightening up the program portfolio, course offerings, schedules, and faculty loads. After a battle with the board, Sue invested the savings in growth. Three new programs enrolled over 150 students. Sue beefed up marketing, especially for five large programs in growing markets. Fall enrollments in the programs were up 10 percent. For the first time in years, overall enrollment increased, and the school ran a surplus.

Yet threats remained. Sue was painfully aware of online competitors enrolling more local students, free community college opportunities, and underenrolled sections and courses creeping back. There were also opportunities for a few new programs. The program portfolio needed another review.

Sue began describing to her cabinet an ongoing management process to sustain curricular efficiency and keep program plans and evaluations up to date.

Her deans erupted.

"You've got to be kidding. We just don't have time for this."

"What do you think has changed?"

"Damn it, this is just what I was afraid of. We are going to run the university like an outlet store, chasing the latest fashion and lowest price."

Dean Harkins stepped in. "I opposed the first project. It seemed like a waste of time and a front for faculty cuts. Instead, it got us on a stable financial footing. For the first time in years, we don't have to lay off faculty or fire adjuncts. We have more time to prepare for fewer classes. Our graduation rates are up. I am for whatever it takes to keep it going."

Sue smiled.

Data-Informed Decision-Making

For decades, tuition, enrollment, and budgets were relatively healthy and growing. Hard data about markets was in short supply, with the exception of employment information. Program economics were seldom available. Judgment, power, imitation, evolving knowledge, interdepartmental deals, and anecdotes underlay many decisions about which programs to start, stop, or grow. As a result, institutions did not develop the skills or culture to use market and financial data to inform program decisions.

Making the cultural shift to more data-informed decisions takes time and effort. It is beyond the scope of this book to cover all the work involved, but a few highlights are shared here.

Check your data. We are familiar with several market analyses and academic economics projects that failed because the data was not credible. There are many potential reasons why. The market data may be at the national or state level for institutions that serve a local area. The folks who conduct the analysis are usually doing the work for the first time in their institution's history. They work on the analysis part-time, causing delays of months or years. They face data that is messy and incomplete. Early drafts of software often contain bugs.

To develop sound data, remember to define your markets and gather data for those specific areas. Be careful not to rely on BLS forecasts (remember, over 80 percent of BLS forecasts are off by more than 50 percent). Check that your published IPEDS data is consistent with the data in your market analysis. Don't confuse competition with competitive saturation (all programs have competition, but only a few are saturated). Be sure the detailed program economics numbers tick and tie with total institutional revenue, faculty cost, faculty counts, and other high-level numbers. Look for outliers and challenge trends that are counterintuitive. Review drafts with people at different levels and from different functions—they may spot different types of errors. General skepticism is also useful.

When a draft is complete, invite the deans and chairs to review the data and encourage them to highlight errors so that you can fix them. Review the market data with your marketing team for errors and to see if they have data that could be useful. This process will improve the quality of the data, develop people's understanding of the analysis, and build trust in the results.

Be modest. As researchers, academics know that data is imperfect. If you present your information as absolute truth, it will invite unhealthy skepticism and encourage faculty to find every error they can. If you are candid about gaps in the data and analyses, they are more likely to trust you and the results. Often, they will suggest useful ways to improve them. Even with the best available data, most academic resourcing decisions still require experience and judgment. Reassure people, especially faculty, that your data should inform decisions, not make them.

Use visual math. Some faculty are mathematical geniuses, others left math in high school, and many have no training in finance. Whenever possible, create charts that make numbers and calculations visually obvious. For example, income statements and margin analyses lend themselves to waterfall graphs, where expenses are shown as downward steps from revenue. Simple bar charts ranking programs, departments, or classes on a given metric are often useful, especially if you add an internal average, external benchmark, or target so that people can quickly see what is over or under the norms (see the following example).

> Reassure people, especially faculty, that your data should inform decisions, not make them.

COST/SCH BY PROGRAM, CLIENT VS. BENCHMARK

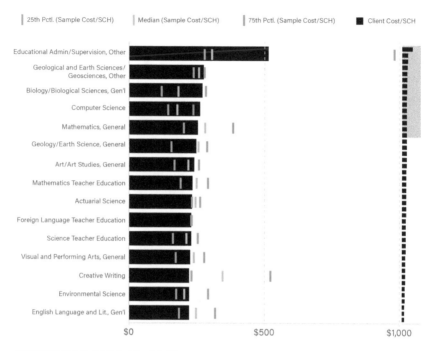

Source: 2021 Gray Academic Cost Benchmarking

Use tables for detailed analysis. Curricular efficiency relies on data at the course and section levels, where visuals may get in the way. For detailed analysis, a well-designed table of the relevant data (e.g., cost per SCH) may be more beneficial. The ability to sort and filter the table on each metric is particularly useful.

Create one-pagers. It is helpful to present the data that decision makers need on one page. Even if it is a little ugly, a summary page saves time, makes the relevant data visible, and increases the chances that it will be considered.

Find the minimum viable product. At the start, the goal is to get useful information for important decisions into the hands of your decision makers. The first round is going to be rough and incomplete, but seeking perfection or answering all questions will doom the project. Think through what Release 1.0 *must* include. The rest can wait.

Maintain and upgrade. Once Release 1.0 is done, the work continues. The data needs to be updated and cleaned up on a regular basis, analytical tools and techniques advanced, and visualizations made clearer. Be sure to allocate some resources to continuously improve the system (or outsource it). In a couple of years, it should be substantially more accurate, comprehensive, and visually appealing than Release 1.0. In the process, faculty and administrators will develop trust in the data, learn how to navigate the systems, and get accustomed to using your data to inform their decisions.

Once you have a clean version of Release 1.0, your faculty, deans, administrators, and others will need to develop an understanding of program data and become willing and accustomed to using it. How will this transformation take place?

A Workshop Approach

In program evaluation workshops, your team can evaluate an entire portfolio of current and potential programs. In two days, they can reach a preliminary data-informed consensus, subject to further assessment, on which programs to start, stop, sustain, fix, or grow. In the workshop, participants gain firsthand experience making data-informed program decisions and can directly perceive the benefits.

WORKSHOP PARTICIPANTS

A successful workshop must have the right participants for the institution. Career and technical colleges are often accustomed to top-down decisions, which may involve a half dozen people. Universities usually need broader participation that may include senior faculty, department chairs, deans, the provost, admissions, marketing, career services, and finance. In many cases, the college president will attend to emphasize the importance of the process. In our experience, it is unwieldy if more than forty-five people participate in the workshop, so larger schools may need to limit the invitees; functional representation and expertise remain important, but more junior participants may be left out. Here are examples of the folks invited to the program evaluation workshop at a large state university and a small private college.

PROGRAM EVALUATION WORKSHOPS: WHO SHOULD BE INVITED?

TITLE OR FUNCTION	LARGE STATE UNIVERSITY	SMALL PRIVATE COLLEGE OR COMMUNITY COLLEGE
Board of trustees	Optional representative	Optional representative
President	President: For kickoff and wrap-up	President: For the entire session
Finance	Senior manager	CFO
Office of the provost	Provost or assistant provost	Provost
Deans	All deans	All deans
Associate deans and chairs	Selected representatives	Selected representatives
Faculty	Faculty senate president Selected faculty senate members Faculty union leader	Faculty senate president Selected faculty senate members Selected senior faculty Faculty union leader (if any)
Institutional research	Department head	Department head
Admissions	Department head	Department head
Marketing	CMO or senior manager	Department head
Student services	Senior manager	Department head
Student government representative	Optional	Optional

WORKSHOP AGENDA

We have conducted over one hundred program evaluation workshops, during which we have developed and refined the agenda. Every workshop takes its own unique twists and turns, but the general outline is illustrated here.

DAY 1 NEW PROGRAMS	DAY 2 CURRENT PROGRAMS
• Present workshop objectives • Summarize approach to program selection • Share initial scoring outcomes • Discuss and refine scoring system • Rerun scores, using refined scoring system • Evaluate proposed programs • Rank and select new programs to Start (after further research)	• Review Day 1 outcomes • Rank current programs • Discuss high- and low-scoring programs • Select programs to Stop • Select programs to Grow • Wrap-Up: Agree on next steps, tasks, owners, and deadlines

The workshop should open with remarks by the president or provost to affirm the workshop's objectives and importance. The remarks should also establish that the group is responsible for the quality of the workshop process and recommendations. After the introduction, Gray Associates or the event leaders describe the market data on student demand, employment, competition, and degree fit.

Often, we have program economics and will explain how they are calculated and what they mean. We then walk through the customized scoring rubric we have prepared with a small client team prior to the workshop. The rubric scores all IPEDS programs, including the school's programs, on over forty metrics (see the following figure). We facilitate a discussion of its strengths and weaknesses, especially its fit with the institution's strategy and current situation. The discussion may lead to real-time adjustments to the scoring thresholds and weights. This conversation enables the group to understand and to take ownership of the scoring rubrics and builds confidence in their results.

PES+ MARKETS: ILLUSTRATIVE SCORING RUBRIC

Bracket	Target Percentile	Assigned Score
High	≥98	8
Medium	≥80	6
Low	≥50	4
Minimum	≥20	2
Zero to Minimum	≥0	0

1. Targets

Using percentiles, we set a performance threshold for each metric. In this case, the threshold for High is the 98th percentile.

Institutions can adjust targets and scores to reflect institutional priorities.

2. Scores

Programs receive scores for reaching a threshold. A program at or above the 98th percentile for Metric 1 would receive 8 points.

At the end of this session, the full group engages in a case discussion of a program scorecard and makes a hypothetical program decision. The discussion of the data, scoring, and case takes about an hour and a half, which is a significant commitment of time. We have tried shortening or skipping the data description, but the time saved is later lost addressing dozens of questions, concerns, misconceptions, misinterpretations, and inaccurate application leading to wrong assessments.

In the afternoon, the workshop turns to identifying potential new programs. We start with new programs because there are hundreds of options to consider, and many are relatively unknown to the institution simply because they do not offer them. This combination makes participants more likely to use data to screen and evaluate options. Emphasizing new programs and growth allays fears that the workshop is just a smokescreen for cutting programs and faculty. It also exposes participants to data on attractive programs, which sets a context for the evaluation of current programs on the second day.

Additionally, selecting new programs is a somewhat less contentious way to get the participants working together and using the data. The discussion begins in small groups, which are tasked with identifying high-potential new programs and sharing their ideas with the full group. The full group discusses the potential programs and agrees on a short list of five to fifteen programs that merit further research and possible approval. The list should be long enough to allow for a few to be eliminated while leaving enough high-quality new programs to achieve the institution's goals.

On the second day, the group evaluates the institution's current programs. If program economics have been completed, they are introduced and explained. The scoring rubric is revisited and may be adjusted to reflect what the team has learned from its use on day one. Small groups then discuss the scorecards on program markets and (if available) program economics. The data may conflict with people's beliefs and values and challenge the viability of their jobs. As a result, this is the most intense and difficult discussion in the workshop, but it is essential to give people the opportunity to candidly discuss the data and its implications. There are several alternatives to organizing the breakout group discussions.

If the program portfolio is relatively small (under a hundred programs), the breakouts can evaluate the entire portfolio and reconcile the findings during the full-group session. Alternatively, each department can evaluate its own programs. The evaluations are then reviewed and revised in the full-group discussion. In some cases, this works quite well, with the full group challenging departmental recommendations that are inconsistent with the data. In other cases, there is tacit agreement not to critique a dean's recommendations for fear they will retaliate against the offending department's suggestions or the individual making the comment.

Personally, I like to have each group assess their own department's programs and the programs of one other department. This approach ensures that each program gets two evaluations. In the full group, we filter for the programs where the small groups agreed. Usually, the full group affirms these decisions fairly quickly. There is then time to discuss the programs where the groups disagreed, which leads to rich conversation. I have to confess that this is usually a longer process, which may spill over into a two- to four-hour session after the workshop. The extra time has not been a major issue if the follow-up meeting is virtual. If it were face-to-face, reassembling the team would be a challenge and a less time-consuming approach may be appropriate.

By the conclusion of the workshop, the participants will have assigned all current and selected new programs to one of five categories: start, sunset, sustain, fix, or grow. For the fixer-uppers, they will have noted the nature of the change, for example, curriculum redesign. It is appealing to put dozens of programs into grow, despite declining markets and enrollment. The first screen should be whether the market is likely to support growth. A declining, highly competitive market is an unlikely spot for a growing program. Program economics are the third screen; in some cases, growth may increase losses. The final screen is whether growth requires incremental investment. Grow should be reserved for a few programs in healthy markets, with attractive economics that require a manageable amount of investment. Most institutions can afford only to fund the growth of five or ten existing programs. To make this distinction clear, it may help to refer to this category as invest and grow.

Very few institutions can make final program decisions in the workshop. More commonly, the workshop findings are preliminary recommendations, subject to further research, review, and approval by the curricular committee, faculty senate, and board.

In schools with powerful deans and responsibility-centered management (RCM) practices, there may be pressure to position the meeting as an exercise or a training session so that the deans can make their own recommendations later without input from their peers. However, two days is a long time to spend in an exercise. If the deans have the power to ignore the results of the workshop, it may be more productive to run a one-day training session, not a two-day workshop.

Program Evaluation Process and Frequency

It is a truism that the pace of change is increasing across our society and industries. This trend does not imply a uniform pace of change across all disciplines, analyzing every program-related topic with the same frequency, or even responding to market changes at all (which can work for a college with a unique brand). Instead, it suggests developing tools and processes that can quickly identify environmental, epistemic, and operational changes and enable fast, sound decisions. Nonetheless, many aspects of academic programs can and should be evaluated more frequently than they usually are.

EVERY SIX MONTHS	EVERY YEAR	EVERY 2–3 YEARS
• Student Demand • Job Postings • Course Enrollment • Course Completion • Short-Term Staffing • Goals, Actions, Status • Competition (online programs)	• Retention • Completion • Economics • Longer-Term Staffing • Curriculum (fast-moving programs) • Competition (online programs)	• Learning Objectives • Student Outcomes • Curriculum (most programs) • Longer-Term Staffing • Resources • Alignment with Mission

PROGRAM MANAGEMENT DASHBOARD

MISSION	ACADEMIC STANDARDS	MARGINS	MARKETS

Student demand moves fast. For example, the pandemic stimulated a surge in psychology and public health. After years of growth, the demand for RN to BSN programs dropped because nurses became too busy to study. Market data on student demand updates monthly (or more often). About once a quarter, or at least once a semester, the provost and deans should scan for material changes in student demand. While these short-term shifts usually should not lead to program changes, they should inform decisions about courses and sections, which will affect staffing and curricular efficiency.

Local employer hiring also changes rapidly. Technology may enable entire industries to expand, such as wind power, e-sports, or artificial intelligence. The government may fund or defund specific industries, such as infrastructure and quantum computing. Local employers may win or lose, even in growing markets. In the 1990s, US solar panel manufacturers in California were abruptly crushed by poor technology decisions and aggressive Chinese competitors. We now know that pandemics can shut down entire industries overnight.

Individual job postings update continuously and should be analyzed immediately if there is a sudden economic change, natural disaster, or disruptive event. In more normal times, for the provost and deans, quarterly updates may identify changes in hiring for graduates and employer-sponsored training. To identify program-level issues and opportunities, annual reviews may be appropriate. In fast-moving disciplines (e.g., computer science), faculty should review hiring trends every year, perhaps even by semester, to identify skills that should be added to or dropped from the curriculum. In more stable disciplines, less frequent skill reviews may be appropriate.

Competition for on-campus offerings moves a little more slowly than employment or student demand. The National Student Clearinghouse data on enrollment by program updates three times a year and is well worth checking for trends. IPEDS completions update only once a year. Clearinghouse data on competition for your applicants is worth checking at least annually in case a particular school is eroding your base. Overall, it is safe to review on-campus competition once a year.

Online competition moves much faster. Provosts, deans, chairs, and marketers need to be up to date every month on new program announcements, competitive advertising, and rising costs per click (a sign of increasing competition). Monitoring job postings for your competition can also reveal where they are growing and if they plan to offer a new program. The Clearinghouse data should be checked when it comes out.

That leads us to program economics and curricular efficiency. The underlying decisions and data change only once a semester. Further, institutions often find it time consuming to pull the data, so most update program economics only once a year. This frequency is likely to change: Revenue, cost, and margin will be expected every semester for each program, department, course, and section. Provosts, deans, and chairs should evaluate the data as often as it becomes available so that they can adjust decisions on courses offered, course frequency, and sections required. Institutions should use academic economics to evaluate each program's vitality on an annual basis.

There are curricular efficiency indicators that can be used more frequently. Enrollment by course and section should be updated before and after the add/drop deadline. Before the add/drop date, some courses with low enrollment may be canceled or postponed

> Institutions should use academic economics to evaluate each program's vitality on an annual basis.

so that they can run full at a later date. Care should be taken to not accidentally delay matriculation for students who need to complete a course to advance in their major. After the add/drop date, underenrolled or overenrolled courses can be flagged so that they are better managed in the next semester. Most of this work should be done by chairs, with deans and the provost setting appropriate guidelines (e.g., the minimum number of students per course or section) and monitoring results. Less-than-degree offerings can usually be expanded or dropped as their economics change; they should be reviewed each time they are offered and before they are offered again.

Many measures of academic performance should also be reviewed annually and sometimes more often. Enrollment, grades of D, F, or withdrawal (DFW rates), semester-to-semester retention, time to degree, graduation rates, and employment are important indicators of student success. They should be tracked not only by program but also by student segment to determine whether the institution, department, program, course, and section are meeting goals for equitable student success. Academic leaders should monitor and improve programs that do not include a healthy representation of men, women, minorities, and Pell-eligible students.

Once a year, the team responsible for a program should address how it relates to the institutional mission and strategic objectives, which may include types of students served, student outcomes, research and scholarship, and effects on the local community and society. This information will guide decisions on whether the program merits institutional support or should generate margin and contribute to the institution as a whole.

Last but not least, chairs and faculty should identify the goals, tasks, responsibilities, and deadlines for program improvement. We suggest quarterly reviews of these action plans so that they are not lost among the many other faculty responsibilities.

Evaluations of this scope and frequency cannot be done by hand. Systems need to populate standardized, clear, and succinct dashboards. Developing this software may seem daunting, but many institutions, like Regis University in Denver, have built their own and others have purchased them. If you do not have these systems in place, you are three to five years behind.

Fortunately, starting out behind has its advantages. Today's management and student information systems make assembling the data much easier. Modern business intelligence tools, such as Qlik, make building dashboards faster. People can now be hired who know how to build the systems, which can save years of work. Working with your team, Gray can implement the systems in three to five months.

The data and systems also need to be maintained. I am always surprised that system maintenance takes as much work as development. It also takes considerable time and effort with your faculty and administrators to refine the data and eliminate subtle errors and departmental anomalies. Dozens of people need careful training on why and how to use the information to make decisions; as people change roles, more will need to be trained, and existing users may need a refresher. Be sure you win the funding needed to sustain the systems and know-how you build.

Organizing for Success

In between accreditation visits and formal program assessments, there may be no one engaged in or responsible for ongoing academic program management and new program evaluation. The skills and tools required may begin to rust and old decision-making habits may reemerge. Putting a few people in charge of the data and process (usually not the decisions) can help to keep data-informed academic program evaluation on track.

ACADEMIC PROGRAM EVALUATION
AND MANAGEMENT ANALYST

Academic program evaluation and management analyst is a useful, part-time role helping faculty use market and economic data to evaluate new program ideas. In a smaller or centralized institution, one person may fill the role for the whole university. If deans are powerful and RCM is in place, program analysts may need to reside in each college, where the role may be filled by an assistant dean, a chair, or a faculty member with an analytical bent. Some of the best program analysts are entrepreneurial and highly analytical faculty members who enjoy using data to search for opportunities. Others may come from finance or institutional research, where they learned how to create, manage, and interpret large data sets.

In the future, as the role matures, academic program evaluation and management analysts are likely to begin surveying existing programs and flagging a few that need attention or reevaluation. They may also be asked to manage the review process for existing programs, ensuring that data is assembled, criteria are defined, meetings are organized, and reviews are conducted. Most importantly, they need to be sure that institutional leaders have the data they need to identify issues, ask informed questions, and challenge glib answers.

Leadership

Leaders at all levels will need to invest time to understand program data and its applications. There are books, like this one, that will help. Gray offers a wealth of other resources. Gray and Bay Path University have launched a course and certificate in Academic Program Evaluation and Management. Gray offers a series of Masterclass webinars, which usually launch in January and continue, once a month, until summer. Gray's website has dozens of white papers and blog posts on program evaluation. Gray's analysts frequently run training sessions for individuals and small groups and host office hours for drop-ins. Once your academic program analysts are in place, they could run classes, briefings, and one-on-one meetings that could help everyone understand and use the data.

The transition to data-informed program evaluation and management will require active support from institutional leaders, especially the provost, and to a lesser degree the board, president, and CFO. The lever for this transition is a cascade of questions and an expectation that the answers are data-informed.

BOARD

In general, it is not the board's role to intrude on operational decisions about individual programs. The board should influence the direction of the program portfolio, the program governance process, and approvals for program investments, which usually includes approval for new programs.

To stay informed about the program portfolio as a whole and its health, the board should receive a summary of program margins, markets, academic performance, and improvement initiatives.

In addition, the board should request a summary of curricular efficiency initiatives and results. For new program proposals, it should require a detailed, consistent program market scorecard and cross-functional business plan (i.e., a plan that includes input, tasks and costs for marketing, admissions, legal, financial aid, academics, and other groups that will need to support the launch).

The board can lead the shift to data-informed program decisions by asking the right questions.

- Which program markets have the fastest growth in student demand nationally and in the markets we serve? Which are in decline?

- Which jobs and skills are in high demand nationally and in the markets we serve? Which are in decline? Which programs lead to careers in these fields?

- Which national jobs can now be performed remotely by local graduates?

- How many of our programs are in the fast-growing fields? Declining fields? What percentage of our students are in these programs?

- What are the overall economics of our program portfolio? What is the median revenue, cost, and margin per SCH? How does this vary by degree level and department?

- How do our economics compare to the results at high-performing institutions? At our peer institutions? How do program and course economics vary within the university?

- What percentage of our programs are more than 50 percent above the median cost per SCH?

- How is the institution going to improve program economics? What initiatives are underway? How are they progressing? What else may need to be done?

- What are the costs for departmental overhead? How does departmental cost per SCH compare across departments? How does it compare with external benchmarks?

The president should receive similar reports and discuss the issues they raise with the board and the provost. The president should be prepared to answer the board's questions and understand the implications for the institution's health. From there, the president's questions become more focused and operational.

- Which of our existing programs are in healthy markets with room to grow? What could we do to accelerate their growth?

- What programs should we launch to take advantage of growth opportunities?

- How should we improve each program to better align it with current knowledge in the discipline, student demand, and employer needs?

- How can we improve each program's economics?

- How can we increase equitable student success in each program?

- Which programs are in weak markets and have poor economics? Are they mission-critical? How can we reduce the institutional resources they need?

- What is a student's return on investment for this program?

- How many courses in this department or program have fewer than ten students enrolled? Should we continue to offer them? Why? How often?

- What departments and courses have the highest cost per SCH? Can their costs be reduced?

Provosts are the linchpin in this change. Provosts can delegate the development of reports and analyses, but they must engage with the data. They should review summary data and program dashboards, make informed observations, and ask questions of the deans, who will then begin asking chairs questions about their programs and courses. Provosts should be politely intolerant of uninformed opinions and request supporting data. In addition to the previous questions, a provost should be probing into the whys underlying the performance of programs and program-related processes. The following are a few of many questions a provost should ask:

- What could we do to increase market share and growth for this program?

- Student demand is rising/falling for this program. How should we adjust staffing?

- This market is growing; should we enter? With a new program or by modifying an existing program to address the opportunity?

- This program market is stable. Why is our enrollment falling? How many completions do our local competitors have? Could we add an online version to increase enrollment?

- The margins on this program are 20 percent above or below our median margin per SCH. Why? What can we learn from it? How can it be improved?

- For all programs, how do retention and graduation rates vary by income and ethnicity? How can we improve them? How do these rates compare to benchmarks at high-performing institutions? What is the program's revenue, cost, and margin per graduate? What is the value of a 1 percent improvement in program graduation rates?

- Too few of our graduates in this program are getting jobs. How many local job postings are there? Can we improve our results? Are there other skills we should teach to make our graduates more successful? If not, should we shrink the program to more closely align with the job market?

The cascade of questions from the board to the president to the provost to deans to chairs and professors will engage the institution in a discussion of the data and its implications. Over time, the questions will become second nature, and people will become reasonably expert in using the data and reports to find the answers. Opinions about programs and their potential will be reframed as hypotheses that can be researched and tested, using simple questions such as "What are the median program completions at other schools?" or "How many job postings are there in our core market?" Questions should also encourage a review of all the relevant data sources, not just one. For example, labor market assertions should be backed up by data from BLS and job postings—not just one or the other.

Leaders also need to carve out time for more frequent program reviews, as outlined previously. The reviews should drive decisions ranging from investment in new programs to improving curricula in existing classes and adjusting faculty loads. Once people understand that information will be used to make these decisions, they will be more likely to gather the data.

The informed, frequent, and sustained focus of leaders on academic program data and performance will improve the quality and efficiency of instruction, lower the cost of higher education, and enable more students to successfully complete degrees. It will begin a shift toward more data-informed discussions and decisions across the institution. It will also improve institutional finances and enable investments in the mission, whether they be adding support to improve graduation rates or sustaining mission-critical small programs.

Program Prediction and Planning

One of the questions that will be asked is, "If we implement this program decision, how will our staffing and financials change?" This is a surprisingly tricky question to answer, because program changes ripple out to all the departments in which a program's students enroll. If we teach fewer engineers, enrollment in English general education courses will fall. The models must consider minimum, maximum, and ideal class sizes—one fewer English student usually will not change the number of English sections that are needed.

Program evaluation trends focus on a snapshot of each program at a moment in time. It may not provide insights on long-term program size and its implications for staffing and specialized facilities, such as lab space. Using IPEDS and other sources, program planning models can be built that estimate future enrollment, revenue, cost, margin, and space requirements.

Trends in IPEDS completions and BLS employment are reasonable places to start. Recent trends can be projected forward for each program and the portfolio as a whole. The trends may need adjustment for the institution's normal growth relative to market in each area. If an institution's psychology program has been growing 10 percent faster than the market for a few years, the market trend might be adjusted up by 10 percent. Since few things grow or shrink forever, institutions may wish to cap growth or decline in programs that are changing very rapidly.

Always keep in mind that trends and predictions are subject to error. It is useful to explore future scenarios to see what the risks and opportunities may be. As we will see in chapter 9, there are analyses you can run to explore the risks and rewards, not just for one program but for the portfolio as a whole.

Dean Harkins continued his quarterly evaluation of the English program. "Student demand continues to decline for humanities programs in general and English in particular. Google searches dropped five percent last quarter, as did National Student Clearinghouse enrollment numbers; our number of new English majors dropped somewhat less and is three percent lower than last semester.

"In response, we have cut a couple of low-enrolled and out-of-date four-hundred-level courses, which were taken primarily by English majors. Of course, the general education courses and lower-level survey courses continue to be popular and generate seventy-five percent margins. We are shifting teaching resources from the higher-level courses to one-hundred-level ones and cutting a few low-performing adjuncts who used to teach one-hundred-level sections. Overall, our instructional cost should drop, and we'll have better professors in front of our students."

"Thank you," Sue said. "How intense is the competition for this program? Are we losing share, or is the market just getting smaller?"

"Let me see," Harkins said as he opened his laptop and looked up the program scorecard. "Actually, competitive intensity seems about average in terms of cost per click and the intensity index. But the average completions per program is dropping. I think the problem is declining interest in the program, not increasing competition."

"That is hard to fix," Sue replied. "Let's continue to be smart about the use of our faculty. I would welcome ideas about how we can revitalize or differentiate the program and get it growing again."

Gray Academic Program Portfolio Strategy

"We focus on doing program analysis one program at a time," Sue said to her team. "But I think a portfolio of programs is more than the sum of its parts. How can we assess the synergies and issues created by the portfolio as a whole?"

A cademic program evaluation and management treats each program on its own merits. Once that is done, academic leaders have a clearer understanding of each program, its opportunity, and its goals. They usually tidy up the portfolio a bit, too, consolidating programs and courses, shutting down a few, and launching new high-potential programs.

A portfolio, or group of programs, is more than the sum of its parts. Academic program portfolio strategy uses two frameworks to assess the portfolio. The first uses program evaluation criteria to assess fit with mission, markets, and margins. The second applies concepts and calculations from modern financial portfolio theory to assess program portfolio risk and growth.

Mission, Academics, Margins, and Markets

As we have discussed throughout this book, academic portfolio strategy starts by using program evaluation criteria—mission, academics, markets, and margins—to assess each program. A portfolio may use high-margin programs that are loosely related to the mission to fund mission-critical programs that consume resources. Institutions may invest to grow high-margin, mission-aligned programs in healthy markets. Overall, this framework should help institutions assess whether their programs, margins, and program resource allocation appropriately advance the mission of the institution.

To sustain the vitality of the portfolio and the institution, it is usually important to have a reasonable proportion of programs with healthy markets and margins (the upper-right section of the following chart). Growth in these programs will offset inevitable declines from programs in weak markets. It is worth experimenting with additional marketing for these programs, which may increase program size and margin; if they are well aligned with the mission, it may also improve mission attainment.

> To sustain the vitality of the portfolio and the institution, it is usually important to have a reasonable proportion of programs with healthy markets and margins

ILLUSTRATIVE PROGRAM PORTFOLIO ANALYSIS

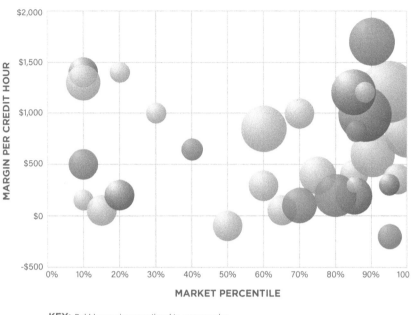

KEY: Bubble area is proportional to program size.
Fill color indicates importance to mission:
Mission-Critical   Mission-Aligned   Discretionary

On the lower right are low-margin programs in healthy markets. The first question to explore in this sector is *why* the programs have low margins. They are in healthy markets and should have room to grow and generate higher margins, but something is holding them back. What is wrong? Is the problem fixable? Sometimes these programs just need investment to grow, improve their margins, and take advantage of their market opportunities. In particular, mission-aligned programs in the lower-right quadrant may merit investments to overcome the constraints on their growth.

The lower left on our chart is the most challenging quadrant. Here we find weak markets and low-margin programs. Because the markets are weak, it is unlikely that these programs will grow. If they have been in decline, they are likely to be overstaffed; cost-cutting may improve their margins. If the programs are not mission-critical, they are candidates to sunset. If nothing is done, the margins on these programs are likely to get worse, drawing more resources that could be better used elsewhere.

The upper left is a sunny corner in a room full of shadows—where the institution has found a way to make money in a weak market. Most likely, these programs should be left to their own devices.

Resource allocation adds another layer to program portfolio management. Behind charts and frameworks that classify programs, leaders need to map and adjust funding by sector. This work should ensure that enough is being spent on growth, supporting large programs, and guaranteeing the survival of mission-critical programs. Most funding should come from successful programs and drawing down resources in declining sectors.

It is important to ensure that large current programs get the resources and managerial attention they need to stay up to date, build positive word of mouth, and produce student outcomes that the institution can be proud of and use in marketing and admissions. However, existing programs, especially large ones, tend to be hungry and have powerful

> Most funding should come from successful programs and drawing down resources in declining sectors.

sponsors, so they may consume more resources than they really need. RCM budgets may intensify this hunger by allowing large, profitable programs and departments to control and consume the resources they create. In contrast, future programs may have no stakeholders and few natural parents or responsibility centers to create or nurture them. Program portfolio leaders need to ensure that programs critical to the future of the institution are also identified and receive appropriate resources and sponsorship.

Nonacademic functions and student support are getting hungrier. Well-funded online competition, enrollment declines, and attempts to expand geographic reach will require more spending on marketing and admissions. Widening gaps in student preparedness, especially among underserved student populations, will increase spending on remediation and student support. Program margins will need to increase to fund these initiatives.

Assessing Risk and Return: Applying Modern Portfolio Theory

Enrollment in some programs may fluctuate widely in response to external factors, such as changes in unemployment rates, while others have steady enrollment. A portfolio of the steady programs may not be exciting, but it may create less institutional risk than a portfolio of volatile programs, unless it includes programs that rise when others fall—leading to consistent overall enrollment. Institutions may have a mission that focuses on an academic sector, such as liberal arts, which increases enrollment risk if the sector falls out of favor. In other cases, rises and declines in enrollment cannot be explained by the program mix; they stem from institutional factors, such as effective marketing or a reputation for educational excellence.

Advanced program portfolio strategy quantifies these general concepts using methods adapted from finance, specifically modern portfolio theory and statistics: beta, correlation, concentration ratios, and company-specific risk.

Beta (β) compares a stock's price fluctuations with the variation in the stock prices for the market as a whole. If a stock were a roller coaster, β measures the height of the peaks and troughs compared to the average roller coaster. A higher β indicates that the roller coaster, or stock, has bigger drops and rises than average. Gray Associates has developed a similar calculation for higher education, βedu which compares the average variability in all IPEDS completions with the variability in completions for a given program. A portfolio of high βedu programs will have greater ups and downs, or risk, than a low βedu portfolio. Going a bit further, it may be worthwhile to look at the volatility of other metrics, such as student demand, enrollment, and employment rates so that institutions can understand the relative risks over the full student life cycle.

Correlation: Some stocks tend to go up and down at the same time; in statistical terms, their movements are positively correlated. This is also true of academic programs. The movement of positively correlated programs will amplify enrollment risk, since they may all go down at the same time. Other, negatively correlated programs go up and down at different times. Negatively correlated programs may reduce risk, since the decline in one program will tend to be offset by an increase in the other.

Sector concentration: Stocks or programs in a sector tend to move in tandem. Engineering programs may go up and down as a group. Having programs or enrollment concentrated in one or a few sectors probably increases risk. As our grandmothers might have said, "Don't put all your eggs in one basket." Sector concentration may have other forms, including concentration by region, student segment, degree level, and modality. A portfolio focused on recent high school graduates will have greater demographic risk (e.g., from a decline in high school graduates) than a portfolio that also appeals to adult learners. As a starting point, it is worthwhile to calculate the percentage of programs, students, faculty, and expenses by four-digit CIP code (which roughly corresponds to an academic discipline).

Company-specific risk: In stock portfolios, once market risks are accounted for, what remains is company-specific risk, or in higher education, institutional or performance risk. This covers a rise or decline caused by the actions of the institution itself. A scandal or weak marketing may cause a decline even in the best of program portfolios. A great brand or a winning football team may attract students despite a weak portfolio.

Program-specific risk: Individual academic programs also have unique risks. As examples, government incentives for completing a specific degree may stop, or a governing body may raise or lower the academic requirements to enter the profession. Many schools offered licensed practical nursing programs that lasted eighteen months or more for full-time students; then the rules changed, and the programs were limited to twelve months of instruction (and much lower revenue). To the extent that a program depends on regulation, accreditation, or state funding, it is subject to abrupt changes at the stroke of a pen. Programs are likely to be more stable if they are linked to longer-term demographic changes (e.g., an aging population), technology (e.g., computer chips get better and cheaper according to Moore's law), or environmental change.

Alpha: The return on a portfolio after accounting for its risk is called alpha. I think of it as the nirvana of portfolio strategy. A high-alpha program portfolio would produce faster growth after accounting for the potential ups and downs of its individual programs.

The beauty of these concepts is that they can be calculated to give insights on the relative health and risk of the portfolio. They can determine whether a portfolio is successful but vulnerable to sharp declines. They help academic leaders and portfolio analysts distinguish between program portfolio issues and poor operational performance. Gray is actively working on these ideas. The following is a simplified example of two real programs with positive alpha (they are both growing) and negative correlation (they go up and down at different times).

The first is for a Respiratory Care Therapist program. On average, between 2010 and 2020, program completions rose 6.6 percent annually. Along the way, though, there were a few bumps: Completions were roughly flat from 2012 to 2014 and declined 4 percent between 2016 and 2018. Then they jumped 15 percent in 2019 and stayed roughly the same in 2020. In its fastest growth year, the program jumped up 15.4 percent; its worst decline was 4 percent. In other words, over the period, growth rates varied by 20 percent, which could be disruptive to institutional financials.[11]

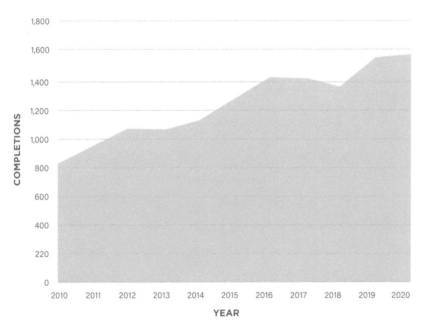

RESPIRATORY CARE THERAPIST
Completions 2010-2020

11   US Department of Education, National Center for Education Statistics, "Integrated Postsecondary Education Data System (IPEDS), 2010–2020 Completions," accessed January 10, 2022, https://nces.ed.gov/ipeds/use-the-data.

The picture for a Cognitive Science program is quite different. Unlike respiratory therapy, cognitive science completions were pretty flat in the early years (2010–2012) and increased sharply every year between 2016 and 2020. Its lowest growth rate was 4.9 percent, and its highest was 35 percent—a thirty-point swing from the lowest to the highest.[12]

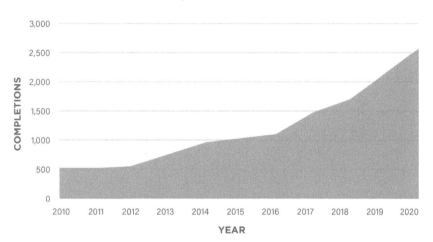

COGNITIVE SCIENCE
Completions 2010-2020

Source: US Department of Education, National Center for Education Statistics, Integrated Postsecondary Education Data System (IPEDS), 2010-2020 Completions

Let's see what happens when you combine the two in one program portfolio.

---

12   Ibid.

VOLATILITY REDUCTION
Respiratory Care Combined with Cognitive Science

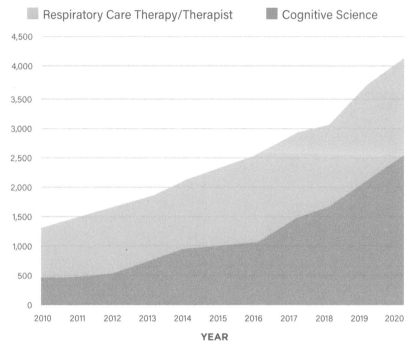

Source: US Department of Education, National Center for Education Statistics, Integrated Postsecondary Education Data System (IPEDS), 2010-2020 Completions

Total completions for the two programs grew every year. The fastest growth was 20.4 percent in 2019, and the slowest was 6.1 percent in 2018. That is only a fourteen-point swing compared to the twenty- and thirty-point swings in the individual programs. By putting two negatively correlated programs in the same portfolio, we reduced volatility and let the CFO get some sleep at night.

Academic program portfolio strategy uses program evaluation criteria to develop and fund programs that produce margin and advance the mission. Modern academic portfolio theory uses measures of growth and risk to drive stable, growing enrollment. In combination, they will increase an institution's mission alpha. They will enable steady, increasing investment in the institutional mission.

It was quite a journey, but Sue had built the systems and culture to support data-informed program decisions and ongoing program evaluation and management. As she said in a conversation with a board member, "I did not realize how far our program evaluation and management had progressed until our recent accreditation visit. We could explain why we had every program, what the issues had been, and how we fixed them. We had hard numbers to show that we had improved and to explain our future plans, including new programs and realignment of our faculty. We had most of the data on program quality at our fingertips. Our quarterly program reviews gave faculty a clear command of the material."

She thought to herself, "And our budget balances every year, despite increasing our spending on our flagship programs. We even managed to keep Dr. Amy Smith, who now leads a thriving humanities department."

Conclusion

The work and expertise required to build academic program evaluation and management systems are substantial. In my experience, enrollment growth, cost reduction, and potential improvements in retention should pay back the development costs many times over. Once the systems and processes are in place, they open opportunities for educators to become academic venture financiers and entrepreneurs.

Provosts will have the data they need to make better decisions on which programs to start, which existing programs to fund and grow, and where to pull the resources needed to pay for these investments. In effect, they can become better academic venture financiers, managing a portfolio of programs that enable institutional growth, reduce risk, and fund education and operations.

Faculty will now have the data to understand markets and economics for hundreds of programs and thousands of certificates. The systems will enable them to find opportunities in almost any field. With this information, institutional leaders and donors will be more likely to fund initiatives, which in turn should generate income for the institution and its departments.

Academics may feel ill-equipped to use the data or take on entrepreneurial roles. Please be assured that while the systems are a challenge to build, they are fairly easy to understand and use. Using the information requires high school-level math (thankfully, not including calculus) and clear thinking. It also requires courage to champion innovative ideas and investment, knowing that even with the best of data, new ideas may fail. Becoming a successful academic entrepreneur is not for the faint of heart—it may take several tries before the program marketing, admissions, content, and outcomes hit the mark.

Here's the catch. Today, all academics are entrepreneurs; some are just more aware of it than others. The competition for academic resources has always been intense. In the future, the growth of human knowledge will continue to outpace funding, higher-education competition will intensify, and the traditional student base will decline. The battle for resources in higher education will only intensify.

> Here's the catch.
> Today, all academics
> are entrepreneurs;
> some are just
> more aware of it
> than others.

The successful academic entrepreneur will improve or build programs that attract students, tuition, and other funding. They will earn the intellectual and economic power to further their research, attract students, develop interesting courses, and retain faculty. They will also differentiate their programs and, in the process, help to differentiate their institutions and build brands that will attract students for years to come. They will attract, educate, and enable generations of students to go on to meaningful careers and become good parents and citizens.

All of this is possible. The journey starts with data-informed decisions that answer the question: What programs should we start, stop, or grow?